Prayers

FOR

KNOWING

GOD

TONY EVANS

HARVEST HOUSE PUBLISHERS
EUGENE, OREGON

Prayers for Knowing God
Copyright © 2021 by Tony Evans
Published by Harvest House Publishers
Eugene, Oregon 97408
www.harvesthousepublishers.com

ISBN 978-0-7369-7534-6 (pbk.)
ISBN 978-0-7369-7535-3 (eBook)

Library of Congress Cataloging-in-Publication Data

Names: Evans, Tony, author.
Title: Prayers for knowing God / Tony Evans.
Description: Eugene, Oregon : Harvest House Publishers, 2021. |
Identifiers: LCCN 2020028994 (print) | LCCN 2020028995 (ebook) | ISBN
   9780736975346 (trade paperback) | ISBN 9780736975353 (ebook)
Subjects: LCSH: Prayers. | God (Christianity)—Knowableness. | God
   (Christianity)
Classification: LCC BV245 .E756 2021 (print) | LCC BV245 (ebook) | DDC
   242/.8—dc23
LC record available at https://lccn.loc.gov/2020028994
LC ebook record available at https://lccn.loc.gov/2020028995

Acknowledgments

I want to thank my friends at Harvest House Publishers for their long-standing partnership in bringing my thoughts, study, and words to print. I particularly want to thank Bob Hawkins for his friendship over the years, as well as his pursuit of excellence in leading his company. I also want to publicly thank Kim Moore and Jean Bloom for their help in the editorial process. In addition, my appreciation goes out to Heather Hair for her skills and insights in collaboration on this manuscript.

Contents

Introduction

K nowing God is the greatest quest you can undertake as a follower of our mighty King. By knowing His heart, His character, and His attributes, you will more fully develop into the kingdom disciple you've been placed on earth to become. You'll also better understand His priorities so you can better align yours under His. And as you come to know God more deeply, you will gain access to many of His benefits, such as peace, grace, guidance, and spiritual prosperity.

In this book, *Prayers for Knowing God*, I've given you a multitude of guided prayers based on God's attributes to help you get to know Him more fully. Numerous of His attributes appear in Scripture, and each one is an expression of who He is and how He relates to you. As you pray these prayers, then, you'll be seeking Him on your own behalf, grounded in the revelation of that particular quality, and you'll come to experience His love and power infused in you on a higher level than ever before. My hope is that your relationship with God will then flourish and overflow, enabling you to live out your purpose of advancing His kingdom agenda on earth.

Prayer is heavenly permission for earthly interference, and it's communication with God, who longs to be involved with you on a very personal level. Prayer opens the door for both that interference and involvement to happen. I want to encourage you, then, to pray regularly, because abiding with God through prayer is one of the most important things you can do in life.

The guided prayers in this book will help facilitate your communication with God. Each one is directed toward one of 55 of His attributes. But they are also crafted to walk you through several of His characteristics simultaneously. For example, the prayer that focuses on God's graciousness includes praise for His mercy. And the prayer directed toward God's attribute of justice includes recognition of His great faithfulness.

As in many other of my guided-prayer books, each prayer has four sections based on the prayer acronym ACTS. This acronym is not a magic formula; rather, it provides structure so our prayers can cover important aspects of communication with God: Adoration, Confession, Thanksgiving, and Supplication.

You can pray these prayers word for word, or you can use them as a springboard to your own prayers directed toward the attributes of God, or you can pray with a combination of the two. It doesn't matter. What matters is that you pray.

I also encourage you to use this book to focus more intently on getting to know God Himself more fully. As you do, you can follow this helpful outline to nurture your time with Him:

> **Identify** a time each day when you can spend concentrated and focused energy on pursuing a greater relationship with God.

> **Consider** several ways to nurture your relationship with God during this time. It could be freely writing thoughts you have toward Him or thanking Him for His attributes in a journal. Or it could be looking up Scripture on a given attribute of God and meditating on it for a few minutes.

> **Evaluate** how your relationship deepens as you spend consistent time with God in His Word and with Him in prayer. Also assess whether praying these prayers makes

it easier for you to proclaim Jesus to others through your words and actions. That should be a natural outgrowth of knowing God's heart more deeply.

Repeat this practice. After you've put it into play for at least a week, continue to incorporate the various prayers into your daily intimate time with God.

I've based many of these prayers on an outline of God's attributes that was first drafted many decades ago for and introduced to the church I pastor, Oak Cliff Bible Fellowship. This outline is included for your reference in Appendix B, and an overview of our national ministry, The Urban Alternative, is in Appendix A. I encourage you to read through both of these before diving into the prayers themselves.

Knowing God will also bring you stability in times of crisis and change. We've gone through a significant number of difficulties and challenges in our culture over the last few years, and everyone could use more calm in their hearts. This guided-prayer book has been designed with the hope that it will bring you just that—calm. As you get to know God through relational communication with Him, may He reveal Himself more fully to you and give you a greater grace and peace each day.

1

Knowing God Through His Holiness

One called out to another and said, "Holy, Holy, Holy, is the LORD of hosts, the whole earth is full of His glory."

ISAIAH 6:3

Adoration

Heavenly Father, I acknowledge Your holiness, and I stand before You in awe of Your holiness. As the angels declared in Your presence, "Holy, Holy, Holy" are You. There is no one like You. No one embodies all of what holiness entails and means but You. You are distinct. You are pure. You are perfect. You are unique. You are separate. You are outside of yet within. You exist in unparalleled measures of holiness.

Today, in my heart, I lift up Your name and the totality of who You are. I exalt You, standing in awe, knowing You alone can claim this title and attribute in its entirety: Holy are You.

Confession

God, I confess that I often don't treat You as Your holiness deserves. It would be easier for me to react to You as I should if You were before me in physical form, because then I would be confronted with Your holiness—either in stature, presence, and power or all of these combined. I would know to stand in reverence or close my mouth in respect. I would know to bow my head as You pass by. But because You are the God who dwells in Spirit and in truth, I often fail to reverence You as I should. I become too easily distracted by life's duties and demands.

Forgive my lack of honor for Your holiness. Forgive me for the flippant manner with which I sometimes approach You or fail to acknowledge just how great, perfect, and powerful You are. Forgive me for fearing what might be rather than fearing You with awe. Let me walk in an increased awareness of Your holiness so that I'll treat You and consider You as I should.

Thanksgiving

Thank You, God, for remaining true and holy. Thank You that, in a world of ongoing degradation of what is moral and pure, You have not changed. You have not diminished Yourself in any way. You have upheld Your holiness amid the cacophony of a broken culture.

Thank You for standing strong in what is right, pure, and holy. Thank You for never wavering, losing it, or misleading those who follow You. Thank You for giving me insight to discern what true holiness looks like and how holiness affects decisions and behavior. Only in my growing and deepening relationship with You will I find the path to personal holiness that will lead me into a life of blessing and favor, according to Your Word (Matthew 5:8).

Supplication

God, Your Word urges me to pursue holiness because You are holy (1 Peter 1:16). According to Your wisdom and Word, guide me into a lifestyle that cultivates holiness both internally and externally in all I do and say. Let my words be few unless they reflect this character of Yours—holiness. Let what I do be done out of a heart that seeks to know You more and aspires to align my ways under Yours.

I ask that Your Helper, the Holy Spirit, nourish, feed, develop, and grow this part of the seed planted in me, which is able to guard and protect my soul from foolish choices (James 1:21). As the angel flew to Isaiah with a coal taken from the fire with tongs to purify Isaiah's lips, let Your Spirit purify and make clean what needs to be purified and cleaned within me (Isaiah 6:6).

In Jesus' name, I pray this prayer asking to know You more through Your holiness. Amen.

2

Knowing God Through His Separation from Sinfulness

All have sinned and fall short of the glory of God.

ROMANS 3:23

Adoration

God, Your glory is the standard. Your perfection and holiness are the bar. I adore You and praise You for being pure and righteous in all things. If there were no perfection in You, there could be no order in the chaos sin brings about. You offer order, mercy, grace, and forgiveness to bridge the gap between humanity's sinfulness and Your holiness.

To know You is to honor the difference between You and me, to recognize that You are the King and set apart. Understanding this lifts my heart to a higher level of praise, because You didn't have to provide a way to close the separation my sin caused between us. But You did, and Your great love provided it so I wouldn't get lost in shame, doubt, darkness, and sin's consequences.

Confession

Heavenly Father, my sin has created a separation between You and me (Isaiah 59:2). I've built barriers to block out the power and flow of Your blessings in my life. I confess to You both sins of omission (neglecting to do what I know is right and good—James 4:17) and sins of commission (intentional action—1 John 3:4). I confess that I fall to my sinful tendencies of selfishness far more than I care to even admit. I confess that I don't show You the love You deserve in my life, nor do I love my enemies as I should.

I confess to both hidden sins and public sins, Lord. I ask that Your Holy Spirit bring to my mind the sins I need to confess to You but have not yet confessed to You. Convict me according to Your Word so I can confess even more. I don't want this separation between us to remain. I want to know You more fully than ever before.

Thanksgiving

Heavenly Father, thank You that sin doesn't have the final say in my life, that it doesn't get to divide You and me and our relationship for all time. Thank You for providing a way for me to know You despite the sins I've committed against You and against humanity. Thank You for bringing conviction to my spirit so that I view and treat my personal sins in a way that honors You—by confessing and repenting in order to pursue the path of purity and holiness, which will bring You glory.

Thank You for keeping me sensitive to Your heart on this subject. In our culture today, it's easy to downplay sin and just call it a mistake or to even marginalize its impact on a person's relationship with You. But however we seek to distort the truth regarding sin to placate our own consciences, I want to thank You for showing me my need to confess, repent, and return to You, acknowledging the truth about sin's destructive nature in my life and in the lives of others.

Supplication

God, draw me close to You through the covering and forgiveness of my sins by the blood of Christ. Make me aware of sin's impact on my thoughts so I can take sinful thoughts captive before they take root and destroy them before they bear rotten fruit in my life (2 Corinthians 10:5). Let me not get lost in the abyss of shame sin seeks to sink me in, but rather show me the way up and out through Your mercy and grace.

I also ask that You help me truly understand and accept Your love so I won't shy away from seeking Your forgiveness of my sins, which I need more than anything else. Show me the tender side of Your heart so I won't allow the fear of punishment to keep me from confessing and repenting of the sins that have held me down (1 John 4:18).

In the name of Jesus, I pray this prayer concerning the separation sinfulness creates and Your addressing that separation through Your love. Amen.

3

Knowing God Through His Forgiveness

The wages of sin is death, but the free gift of God is eternal life in Christ Jesus our Lord.

Romans 6:23

Adoration

Lord God, You gave the gift of life to each one of us through the sacrifice of Your Son, Jesus Christ. And because of Your great love, we have found the way to bridge the separation sin creates.

The sinlessness of Christ as our atoning sacrifice has given us the opportunity to know You. This is a foundational attribute for which I praise and adore You. Without Your loyal love made manifest through this sacrifice on our behalf, none of us could get to know You. The veil has been torn in two so we can enter into Your presence.

Prior to the loving and sufficient sacrifice of Jesus, we had no way to enter into the Holy of Holies apart from animal sacrifice and being chosen to do so at a specific point in time. But from the heavens, Your love reached down into the sinless humanity and deity of Jesus Christ to give me a way to know You each moment of each day. You are near, not far, and I give You praise, honor, and glory for the greatest gift of all: eternal life and the joy of knowing You while yet on earth.

Confession

God, confessing my sins to You gives me the opportunity to be forgiven by You. I confess my sins to You now. But I also want to confess that I don't always take the separation sin produces seriously. Because You have provided the way for me to be forgiven, I sometimes get into the habit of expecting Your forgiveness and taking it for granted.

I confess this to You today, and I ask that You make my heart sensitive to the reality of what Your gift of eternal life really means. Give me a greater glimpse into the very heart of Jesus Christ and the sacrifice He made so I could be forgiven and brought near to You.

Thanksgiving

God, thank You for the free gift of eternal life that came at great cost to You. It cost me nothing. In fact, because it cost me nothing, I sometimes fail to treat it with the honor and gratitude I should. Forgive me for this. But accept my heart of thanks right now so I might know You more closely than ever before.

Show me the hope that comes in recognizing the magnitude of the gift of eternal life You have given through Your Son, Jesus Christ. Thank You that I'm not doomed to a life of separation on earth and eternally in hell. Thank You that the blood of Jesus covers and washes away all of my sins, not just certain ones. Thank You for the power of Your love, which crossed the divide between us my sins had caused and drew me near to You by the grace and mercy of Christ.

Supplication

God, I want to live in the freedom Your gift of life has truly given me. I don't want to live continually looking over my shoulder, waiting for the hammer to drop or hiding in guilt, shame, or doubt. Show me what it means to completely embrace the gift of eternal life given to me, that opened the path toward pursuing knowing You more fully.

Help me come boldly to Your throne because the price was paid for me on Calvary. Show me what it means to let go of guilt, regret, remorse, shame, blame, and disappointment in myself. Show me instead the joy that comes from knowing You are loving and gracious in all Your ways. You demonstrated this first and foremost at the cross in the Person of Jesus Christ. Help me to know that Christ is the foundation of my relationship with You, and help me to always abide in His love.

In Jesus' name, I pray this prayer in pursuit of knowing You more through Your forgiveness. Amen.

Knowing God Through His Mercy

*He saved us, not on the basis of deeds
which we have done in righteousness,
but according to His mercy,
by the washing of regeneration and
renewing by the Holy Spirit.*

TITUS 3:5

Adoration

God, to know You is to know Your mercy, because without Your mercy, I can't approach You to get to know You. You are the great, supreme King who rules over all, judging all things according to Your righteousness, and if not for Your mercy, I would have been judged long ago. Instead, I've been given the chance to pursue a life of meaning, purpose, and influence through my intimate connection with You as the Source and provider of all.

When it's my role to show mercy to someone who has betrayed me or even simply dismissed me, however, I find it hard to do. Something inside me resists. But Your mercy flows like the water cascading over the rocks of a waterfall. There is no resistance. You hold nothing back. You wash each of us clean with Your love, and I praise and adore You for Your ability to show mercy where it's undeserved.

Confession

God, too often I fail to recognize, acknowledge, or thank You for the countless things in my life to which Your mercy is applied. So many times You have withheld Your wrath, brought on by my sinful choices, and I have come to expect Your mercy. But mercy is never to be expected. Mercy is the gift of the Giver.

I confess to You that, as someone given this great gift of mercy over and over again, I don't always honor You in my heart. I focus more on myself and my agenda than on advancing Your kingdom agenda through my words and actions. Forgive me for failing to respond to Your mercy in such a way that makes me a full-on kingdom steward and kingdom disciple, both overall and in all that I do.

Thanksgiving

Heavenly Father, thank You for the depths of Your love from which flows Your great mercy. Thank You for the power of Your patience that allows You to respond with such lovingkindness in the face of my sins. Thank You for reminding me of Your mercy so that I don't grow complacent.

Your mercy serves as a motivator for me to serve You and love You all the more. Thank You for caring for me so much that You want me to serve You. Thank You for believing in me and for using me in advancing Your kingdom agenda on earth.

Supplication

God, I want to know Your mercy more. I want to realize how much You've shown me already. I don't want to overlook the level and depth of mercy You have shown me over the course of my life. I believe that a real reflection on Your mercy to me will cultivate in me a greater level of thankfulness. Grow this gratitude in me as a response to Your great mercy.

In the name of Jesus, I ask to know You more through knowing Your mercy. Amen.

Knowing God Through His Grace

Let us draw near with confidence to the throne of grace,
so that we may receive mercy and find grace to
help in time of need.

HEBREWS 4:16

Adoration

God, I lift up Your name in praise and honor. You have enabled me to approach You out of a heart of confidence because of the saving work of Jesus Christ. Your mercy and Your grace open the door of entry into Your throne room so I can access even more of Your mercy and grace. You have provided both the key and the prize the key unlocks. I worship You for Your all-sufficiency, which enables You to do just that.

I honor Your name because You are above all and because Your grace provides me with what I need to carry out Your will and purpose in my life. Let my praise bring You pleasure through this prayer.

Confession

God, I know Your grace rains down as a flood, and yet I confess that I don't tap into its power nearly as much as I should. I confess that I far too often live my life looking over my shoulder for Your anger or disapproval rather than running to You with arms open wide to be fully embraced by Your grace.

Forgive me for my hesitation, out of my fear, to know You as intimately as You have made it possible for me to know You. Fear denies the existence of grace or, at a minimum, it devalues it. Forgive me for doubting Your grace rather than diving into the depths of the love Your grace provides.

Thanksgiving

Heavenly Father, thank You for the abundant supply of Your grace. Thank You for loving me so much that Your grace is available to me at all times. Thank You for Your presence in my life, which reminds me of the constant gift of grace. Grace fills the gaps where I'm lacking, enabling me to fully maximize my potential and purpose for Your kingdom agenda on earth. Thank You for gifting me with spiritual gifts I can tap into because of Your grace. Thank You that Your grace is greater than all of my sin.

Supplication

God, I want to know all that You have preordained for Your grace to accomplish in my life. I don't want to fall short of Your grace in any way. Give me wisdom and insight for how to align myself under Your rule in such a manner that will unlock the power of grace in my life.

Show me how to benefit from this enormous gift. Make me not only a mouthpiece for Your Word and Your values but also a conduit for delivering Your grace to those who need it. May I reflect the grace You have shown me in how I treat others, and I ask that all my words be seasoned with this greatest of gifts, Your grace (Colossians 4:6).

In Jesus' name, I pray this prayer in my quest to know Your grace more completely. Amen.

Knowing God Through His Redemptive Power

*I have wiped out your transgressions
like a thick cloud and your
sins like a heavy mist.
Return to Me,
for I have redeemed you.*

Isaiah 44:22

Adoration

Holy God, I worship You for Your redemptive power. I honor Your name and come to You in order to draw close to You in praise and adoration. The strength of who You are shines through in the ability You have to redeem what was lost and to restore what has been destroyed by the evil one.

Let my praise ring loudly in Your ears, and let Your heart receive my gratitude with joy. Show me how to display my honor of You in even more ways than through prayer. Show me how to delight You with my praise for how You have redeemed me from the pit and crowned me with loving devotion and compassion (Psalm 103:4). Your compassion knows no boundaries. Your redemptive arm knows no length that extends beyond it (Isaiah 52:10).

Confession

God, I confess to You my lack of awareness of how much You have redeemed me from. I confess that I go about my days without paying much attention to the level of love You have shown me through Your redemption. It's easy to look at ways I need You to rescue me but then glance over the negative consequences that come about due to my sins and dismissal of Your rightful rule in my life. Yet You have redeemed me from both what others have caused me due to their sin and what I've caused myself due to my own sin.

I confess to You my failure to thank You and honor You for Your redemptive hand in my life as much as I should, based on what You have done to set me in a high place above that which Satan used to seek my harm (Psalm 27:5).

Thanksgiving

Father, thank You for Your love. Thank You for Your ability to turn things around through Your redemptive power. You can create a U-turn where it looks like I've become lost. You can break the chains that bind me. Thank You for knowing I am but dust and yet taking that reality into consideration with Your love (Psalm 103:14). You are mindful of me and willing to redeem me because of Your great awareness of my limitations combined with Your great love.

I also give You thanks for Your strength—strength that covers me when the enemy seeks to come at me with a storm. Strength that hides me in the shelter of Your wings (Psalm 91:4). Strength that shows me the path to take (Psalm 25:4).

Thank You for all of these things You use to redeem me and restore me to a right relationship with You.

Supplication

God, show me how to let go of my shame and regret as You have done in redeeming me. You have wiped away my sins like a cloud, and yet I still hold on to the aftereffects of my sin. Show me how to love myself as fully and compassionately as You do. Your redeeming power has brought me hope; but let me not cut short that hope in failing to walk fully in what Your redemption has allowed.

I want to hold up my head in the confidence that redemption supplies. Help me not cut short the manifestation of Your will in my life due to a failure of mine to embrace, receive, and maximize Your redemptive power. I want to know the heart of love You have for me that has allowed You to show me so much mercy, grace, compassion, and redemption. I want to know You more.

In the name of Jesus, I pray this prayer, asking to know You more through Your redemptive power in my life. Amen.

7

Knowing God Through His Desire for My Personal Holiness

It is written, "YOU SHALL BE HOLY, FOR I AM HOLY."

1 PETER 1:16

Adoration

God, Your desire for my personal growth and holiness stems from Your great love for me. You know that by growing in spiritual maturity and holiness, I will be able to tap into a deeper intimacy with You. You are holy, and those who share a close fellowship with You walk in Your holiness as well.

I praise You for Your desire to always see me becoming the best version of myself according to Your will and perfect plan. I adore You for the power You make available to me so I can live a life of holiness. You have placed within me all that I need to live a life of godliness (2 Peter 1:3). I worship You for Your provision of goodness and how that draws me closer to You in every way.

Confession

Heavenly Father, I confess that I am not holy as You are holy. I desire to be. I want to be. I strive to be. But I fall short. I confess my selfishness and self-absorption and how both keep me from living a holy life according to Your kingdom rule of love. I confess that I pay far more attention to my wants and needs while neglecting what other people need or even what You want me to do with my time, my talents, and my treasures. I am sorry, and I do want to do better.

Forgive me for falling short. Forgive me for laziness, greed, jealousy, envy, hate, bitterness, pride, and more. Forgive me for these things that keep holiness from truly manifesting itself through my life as Your kingdom disciple.

Thanksgiving

God, thank You for calling me to a life of holiness. Thank You for caring enough to lift me higher than I ever knew was possible. Thank You for not tossing me aside because of the sins in my life—sins of pride, selfishness, and a lack of love for others. Rather, You ask me to repent and return to You; in You I will find the path to the holiness You have called me to live out. Thank You for giving me a second and third chance, and then even more.

Holiness is the goal for my life, and I want to embody all of who You are so I can share Your love and holiness with others. Thank You for making Yourself available to nurture and guide me as I grow.

Supplication

Lord, make me holy. Make me pure. Make my thoughts fixate on those things that are true, honorable, lovely, and of Your kingdom values. I ask You to help me take captive every thought contrary to Your holiness and truth and cast it away. I ask You to convict me at the very thought or onset of a sin, giving me more than enough space to change my mind and not take part in that which will stain me.

I want to live a life that brings You great joy. Help me do that by Your Spirit's power. Help my thoughts and actions reflect Your holiness to such a degree that I reflect You. I am an image bearer of Yours—made in the image of God. Let my character resemble You, Lord, so that I honor Your name as Your kingdom follower.

In the name of Jesus, I pray this prayer, seeking to be holy as You are holy. Amen.

8

Knowing God Through His Help in Spiritual Growth

I will ask the Father, and He will give you another Helper,
that He may be with you forever.

JOHN 14:16

Adoration

God, I praise You for Your ability to provide all I need to know You more. You have given me the Holy Spirit, whose presence in me allows me to grow and develop spiritual maturity. I worship You for Your tender care that gave me the gift of a Helper.

Your Spirit shows me the way and the path to personal development. Your Spirit convicts me of the areas in my life where I need growth. You have not only called me to spiritual growth but equipped me with all I need to live it out so I can experience You more fully and know You more deeply. I love You and praise You for Your loving care. Receive the praise and adoration of my lips and my life as I lift Your holy name with all honor and glory and praise.

Confession

Heavenly Father, I have all I need to grow in the grace and knowledge of the Lord Jesus Christ and mature spiritually as manifested by the fruit of the Holy Spirit. Yet I often rely on my own insights and my own efforts rather than discover the peace and freedom that come through dependence on Your Spirit in all things.

Forgive me for my independent mind-set that prevents me from growing as I should, according to all that You have given to me in the power of the Spirit. Forgive me for skipping time I should be spending with You in cultivating intimacy with the Spirit so I can learn how to hear the voice of God guiding and directing me in all things. I ask for Your forgiveness for my failure to lean into You as much as I should in order to tap into the power of the Spirit that produces growth and maturity in me.

Thanksgiving

Thank You, God, for the gift of Your Helper, the Holy Spirit. Thank You for showing me that the path to maturity comes through the simplicity of abiding in Your Spirit and hearing Your voice. Thank You for desiring maturity to be produced in me. You have given me all that I need to develop into a mature kingdom disciple. Thank You for Your patience with me as I discover more ways to tap into that power, which comes through a personal knowing and abiding in the Spirit. I thank You for Your provision, Your presence, and Your power, which all enable me to grow in my knowledge of You and in my relationship with You.

Supplication

God, help me grow and develop into a mature kingdom disciple. Help me learn to look to Your worldview and perspective before I look to anything else. I ask for the Helper to give me eyes to see the spiritual side of things rather than what is only on the surface. Show me the areas of my life where I need greater grace, more patience, a deeper understanding of Your goals. Develop in me the muscles of mercy and the heart of hope. In these two things, I will be more firmly rooted and grounded in Your kingdom principles and abounding fruit for my life.

Let me see the benefits of spiritual maturity, for as I witness them, they will serve as motivation for pursuing spiritual growth all the more.

In Jesus' name, I pray this prayer, asking to know You more fully through the role the Holy Spirit plays in my life. Amen.

9

Knowing God Through His Word

This book of the law shall not depart from your mouth,
but you shall meditate on it day and night,
so that you may be careful to do according to all
that is written in it;
for then you will make your way prosperous,
and then you will have success.

JOSHUA 1:8

Adoration

God, Your Word is a light to my path and a guide for my life choices. I adore You and give You praise for providing me with this road map that shows me which way to go. I worship You for the way You put Your Word together over the course of so many years, through so many authors, and yet it remains true in every way.

How You have communicated with us in order to give us guidance in life amazes me. The fact that You provided us with Your Word so we don't have to learn lessons in life the hard way reflects Your great care and compassion for each one of us. I praise You for this great care and compassion, and I honor Your heart as You have sought to honor ours through this life-saving and life-giving tool of Your holy Word.

Confession

God, Your Word is right there, available to me and filled with all of the wisdom I need to live my life to the fullest and escape many of the traps we fall into as people. Yet I confess I don't go to Your Word or use it as I should. I confess that, at times, I even neglect it altogether.

Forgive me, God, for failing to make use of this great gift of Your Word as I should. Forgive me for spending more time on frivolous activities or fun than on the pursuit of knowing You fully through Your revelation in Your Word. Forgive me for not taking up the sword of the Spirit when the enemy comes against me as You have instructed me to do. Your Word gives life, and yet I spend sometimes too little time in it—meditating, memorizing, and applying it. Please have mercy and compassion on me.

Thanksgiving

Heavenly Father, thank You. Thank You for the 66 books of the Bible, which have been handed down throughout time to be a guidepost for my life. Thank You for the Holy Spirit's power to translate and illuminate what You are saying in Your Word to me. Thank You that at any moment in time, I can pick up Your Word and receive insights into Your heart.

Thank You, too, for all of the people who have spent time translating Your Word from the original languages into a language that's easy for me to understand. Thank You for all the people You have called to write commentaries on various passages so I can understand what You are saying all the more. Thank You for protecting and preserving Your Word through the ages and making it so accessible to me as it is right now.

Supplication

God, I can get to know You through Your Word when I take the time to explore, experience, and enjoy the collections You have placed within it.

Give me a heart to know You more. Give me a hunger for Your Word. Increase in me a thirst for illumination and insight. Show me how I can use other tools like commentaries to help me understand things like context, culture, and original intent.

Place me in a Bible-believing and Scripture-honoring community both at church and in community groups. Give me courage to read Your Word more frequently, knowing I may not understand everything at first but that, with my diligence, You will reveal Your meaning to me. Help me exchange entertainment time for time studying Your Word to whatever degree I can. Show me the benefits of knowing You so that I will seek to know You all the more.

In the name of Jesus, I pray this prayer concerning Your Word and its power to help me know You more fully. Amen.

10

Knowing God Through His Infiniteness

He is before all things, and in Him all things hold together.
COLOSSIANS 1:17

Adoration

God, You are the infinite God. You existed before time, and You exist outside of time. You exist after time as well. In You all things are held together. Were You to let loose of Your order over all for even a moment, we would unravel and come to immediate ruin and destruction. We're at Your mercy for every moment of our lives because You hold our lives in Your hand.

I praise and honor You for how great You are and how powerful is Your mighty arm. I worship You for Your ability to know all things, see all things, be over all things, and keep all things working together for Your good and Your glory—especially in my life when I seek You.

Confession

God, please forgive me for my self-limited understanding of You that also limits my awe and worship of You. When Isaiah was taken up to the throne room filled with angels singing Your praise, he became instantly humbled. He knew he was unclean just by getting a glimpse of Your glory and infinite presence.

I confess that I often think too highly of myself because I'm focused on what I can know through my five senses rather than on the spiritual realm, which has You at the head of all things. I ask that You forgive me and show me Your great compassion.

Thanksgiving

God, thank You for Your awesomeness and great power. Thank You that I never have to worry about whether You will supply me with oxygen or even the ability to use that oxygen for my body. Thank You that when I go to sleep, I can trust that You will continue to hold all things together.

Thank You for giving me a greater awareness of how great You are. Because of You, I'm able to enjoy my life. Because of You, I'm able to live out my divine reason for being. And because of Your overarching rule and infiniteness, my own dreams and desires can expand beyond my limited mind-set, reaching into the realm beyond the borders of body, mind, and spirit. With You, anything is possible, because You are over all. Thank You for helping me realize that and reach further than I ever thought possible in my hopes and pursuits.

Supplication

God, I want to know Your infiniteness on a grander scale. Open my heart and mind in such a way that I can experience more of who You are. Help me see beyond what I can see. Help me take steps of faith while trusting that You are before all things and You hold all things together. In this way, I can trust You more and come to know You more.

Increase my awe of You. You deserve my awe and wonder. Increase my awareness of You in every moment of my waking hours so I can experience You more fully. Let the Holy Spirit teach me how great and grand You truly are and how all things rest in Your ability to keep them together. Give me a greater dependence on You to lead me and guide me, because in Your infinite awareness, You know which way I should go.

In the name of Jesus, I pray this prayer, asking to know You more deeply through Your infiniteness. Amen.

11

Knowing God Through His Honesty

By two unchangeable things in which it is impossible for God to lie,
we who have taken refuge would have strong encouragement
to take hold of the hope set before us.

HEBREWS 6:18

Adoration

God, honesty is a rare trait. So much in our world is built on deception, and this reality puts many of us into a state of skepticism or doubt. Yet You are honest. In fact, it is impossible for You to lie. Your truth serves as a refuge in a confusing and ever-changing society.

I adore You and worship You because of the hope I can have in light of Your honesty. I praise and worship You, my God, for giving me the encouragement and rest I need in order to look to You with full confidence. I don't need to question what You say because Your truth is intrinsic to Your very being. Take pleasure in the praise I give You as I take pleasure in the peace I can have in counting on You to always be truthful.

Confession

God, doubt offends Your heart. When I question You or look for ways You may not be telling the truth, I hurt You. I'm sorry. Faith is carrying out actions that demonstrate belief that You are telling the truth. The opposite of faith in You is unbelief in You—not only in what You say but in the character of who You are.

Forgive me for doubting You. Forgive me for failing to put my total trust in You. Show me how to increase my faith. Clean me of the residue that unbelief creates on the inside of me. I want to live with complete faith in You, so please help me do that as You strengthen me and my belief in Your Word.

Thanksgiving

Lord, thank You that I can count on You. Thank You for not causing me to doubt You through Your actions; instead, they cause me to trust You. My doubt comes from my own questions and concerns, but You remain faithful even when I don't live in a full state of faith.

Thank You for remaining changeless in an ever-changing world. Thank You for the consistency of Your truth. Thank You for the authority of Your Word. Thank You that I can count on You to do what You say You will do. I can rely on You for all that I need, based on the promises of Your Word. Thank You for reminding me of this through Scripture and for giving me the opportunity to understand Your Word.

Supplication

God, I ask that You create in my life situations and scenarios where I need to trust You. Walk me along the pathway of faith. Direct my steps so that I intersect with Your truth in order to increase my faith. Show me Your heart so that, when I don't trust Your hand because I can't understand the circumstances surrounding me, I will trust Your heart.

You are truthful and kind. Make it so I will never forget that. As the apostles asked You to do in Luke 17:5, increase my faith. And as the father of a sick child asked You to do in Mark 9:24, help my unbelief. Turn my doubt into a confident trust in Your truth as I look to You to both supply and meet my faith in You.

In the name of Jesus, I pray this prayer in pursuit of knowing You more fully through Your truth and trustworthiness. Amen.

12

Knowing God Through His All-Sufficiency

Just as the Father has life in Himself,
even so He gave to the Son also to have life in Himself.

JOHN 5:26

Adoration

God, my Father, in You is the sufficiency I need to live according to Your perfect will. You are the One who guides and directs me in the way I should go, and I praise You and honor You for the greatness of who You are. You lack nothing. You need nothing. You are dependent upon no one. You are complete, whole, perfect, righteous, mighty, strong, and wise. With my heart I lift up Your name to glorify You in all that I do.

Make my life a living testimony to Your all-sufficiency so I can truly know and honor You through my words and actions. Life itself depends on Your supply. You supply the rain, the sun, light, and life to all who need it. May You receive the praise due Your name.

Confession

God, it's easy for me to become complacent, and in so doing, to ignore the sufficiency found only in You. When I don't think I need to depend on You because I'm unaware of my need, I ignore the rightful place You should have in my life.

Show me how to better honor You even when I feel self-sufficient. Remind me of the connection I have in You, which supplies my very life. Forgive me for failing to thank You and honor You as I should, in such a way that reveals a true understanding and awareness of my dependence on You for everything. In times of testing and trial, this dependence on You comes to life in my heart. Forgive me for my arrogance in times of blessing.

Thanksgiving

Thank You, God, that when I'm in need or lack anything, I can turn to You, and You will supply all that I need. You have said You will never forsake me, so I trust in Your loving hand to supply what I need to sustain life itself.

Thank You for the sunshine that gives life to the land and produces food for us all to eat. Thank You for filling me with good things, Your blessings from above. Thank You for never forgetting me. Thank You that even when times are tough and trials come upon me, You are there to guide me to what I need most. Thank You for the wisdom You supply and the gifts You give, which enable me to move forward in the calling and purpose You have given me.

Supplication

God, help me understand more fully what it means to depend on Your all-sufficiency. Keep me from a proud heart, which lacks discernment as to where all things originate. I humbly bow before You, and I want to honor You in all that I do.

Show me what I can do that will bring You the honor You deserve since You are my Source for all things. Make me know Your full sufficiency—let me taste and see that You are good and that You surely supply all my needs according to Your great riches in glory.

In Christ's name, I ask these things according to the perfect sufficiency of who You are. Amen.

13

Knowing God Through His Faithfulness

Know therefore that the LORD your God, He is God,
the faithful God, who keeps His covenant and His lovingkindness
to a thousandth generation with those who love Him
and keep His commandments.

DEUTERONOMY 7:9

Adoration

God, You are faithful. You keep Your covenant and Your lovingkindness to a thousand generations of those who love You and keep Your commandments. Your faithfulness is like the dew in the morning, giving life to all that it waters. Your faithfulness supplies me with all I need to live out the purpose You have given me.

Your faithfulness sets You apart from all others, letting us know that You alone are God and that You alone are worthy of all praise, all adoration, and all glory. Your name is great, and Your faithfulness is true. I look to You in times of trouble, knowing that Your faithfulness isn't dependent on me but rather on the intrinsic character that embodies Your love in all things. I praise You for Your grace, Your mercy, and Your faithfulness.

Confession

God, I depend on Your faithfulness, especially when I'm not faithful to

You. And in those times I don't pursue knowing You as I should, I still look to You to supply all I need. Yet You remain faithful.

I confess to You that I don't always seek You as I should. I don't always give You the undivided attention and adoration You deserve. I confess I even doubt Your faithfulness and Your Word when troubles and difficulties surround me. Forgive me for fearing when I should be trusting in Your faithfulness. Forgive me for worrying when I should be resting in the reality of Your faithfulness. Forgive me for questioning Your faithful love and provision rather than honoring You with my faith in You.

Thanksgiving

Father, thank You that Your faithfulness isn't dependent on my obedience to You or even on my faith. Thank You that You remain faithful and true even when I forget how faithful You are and give in to worry.

You were faithful to Peter when he stepped out onto the sea. Even though he took his eyes off You and began to sink, You reached out Your hand in faithfulness to lift him from his certain demise. I know I can depend on You always because of Your faithfulness. Thank You for Your great love, which gives me all I need each day.

Supplication

God, I want to honor You with my faith in Your faithfulness. I want to please You with how I respond to difficulties and trials that come my way. I ask that You strengthen my faith and embolden my trust in You so I can bring You glory in all I do and say.

I ask for greater faith in Your faithfulness. I ask for a greater awareness of Your loving hand. I look to You to supply me with all I need, according to Your great faithfulness. Let the light of Your love and faithfulness shine brightly on me, lifting me out of the darkness of despair and into the light of Your love.

In the great name of Jesus Christ, I pray all these things concerning Your great faithfulness. Amen.

14

Knowing God Through His Strength

Who is the King of glory? The LORD strong and mighty,
the LORD mighty in battle.

PSALM 24:8

Adoration

Dear God, You are the King of glory, and You are strong and mighty. You are mighty in battle. Your strength overpowers all who come against You, and I find strength when I rest in the reality of Your strength.

Show me Your mighty arm in battle. Show me how to recognize Your strength so I can gain confidence in relying on You. Set my heart at rest in this very moment, knowing that Your strength is sufficient for all I need. When I look to others for strength, their strength never compares to Yours. My hope is found in no one but You. I praise, worship, and honor You today by acknowledging You are the King who is stronger than all else.

Confession

God, sometimes I think I'm stronger than You. No, I don't place myself in comparison to You and assume I win; rather, I simply rely on my own strength rather than depending on Yours. I wouldn't do that unless somehow and in some way I felt I was stronger than You.

Forgive me for neglecting to depend on Your strength and falsely assuming that my strength is enough for me. Forgive me for forgetting who is God and who is not. You are God, and I am not. I confess my sins of self-sufficiency, pride, and lack of true reliance on You or recognition of You as the Source of my strength. When I face the enemy in battle, forgive me for suiting up in my own armor rather than in the armor You supply, which is all I need for victory.

Thanksgiving

God, receive my thanksgiving out of a heart of humility. Thank You for showing Yourself strong in all things. Thank You that You are great, strong, mighty, and powerful. Your Word is strength to my bones and life to my soul. Help me show You how thankful I am. When worries seem to suck the life from me, help me rest in the awareness of Your power and strength.

Thank You that I can depend on You and that You are ever present in my life. Thank You for supplying all of my needs according to Your riches in glory. Thank You that Your strength is enough for me to find rest in. Thank You for Your willingness to share Your strength with me, for making it available to me at all times if I will just ask You to manifest Your strength in me and through me, according to the faith I've placed in You.

Supplication

God, I ask for Your great power and strength to show Yourself strong in my life and actions. Let Your strength be a calming force in my spirit so I may walk in the shoes of peace. Help me recognize Your strength in me so I can learn how to depend on You more fully.

I pray for wisdom on how to access Your strength regularly for all I need to do. Increase Your strength in me, Lord, so I can walk in Your strength. When others are in need and looking to me for help, give me the strength I need to do that in Your name. Keep me calm in crisis, peaceful in uncertainty, and strong when troubles come because I've learned to access Your faithful strength in all things.

In Jesus' great name, I praise You and thank You for who You are and the strength You supply. Amen.

15

Knowing God Through His Sovereignty

*Keep the commandment without stain or reproach
until the appearing of our Lord Jesus Christ,
which He will bring about at the proper time—
He who is the blessed and only Sovereign,
the King of kings and Lord of lords.*

1 Timothy 6:14-15

Adoration

God, You are the blessed and only Sovereign. You are the King of kings. You are the Lord of lords. Nations rise up against You, but You squelch them in their path. Rulers raise their armies against You, but You rout them as the Lord of hosts over the heavenly army. Satan's minions make their plans to defeat You while You wait for them to make their move, only for You to once and for all shock them into the awareness that You indeed are the Sovereign over all.

While we may attribute glory, honor, or power to people, only You rule. Heaven rules the affairs of men. I give You praise, honor, and glory as I recognize that Your hand is the hand that shapes the destinies of all of us, even though we may not realize it in the process. Mankind can make our plans, but the Sovereign determines the path.

Confession

God, You know more than I how many times I try to rule over my own choices and life path. For a while, You will allow me to feel as if I'm in control. But You, O God, are ultimately in control.

I worship You because I know I can confess my sin to You, all the while trusting that in Your sovereign rule lies Your ability and willingness to forgive me for my sins. Thank You for Your forgiveness, especially in those areas where I try to outsmart You. I can't outsmart You because You are sovereign, all-knowing, and all-powerful. Rather, on my knees, I repent and bow before You, the sovereign King and ruler over all.

Thanksgiving

God, thank You that I don't have the weight of the world on my shoulders. That would be too much for me to bear. Thank You that I don't need to be the one to solve every riddle or defeat every foe. That is Your role as the Sovereign over all. Thank You that Your mercy allows room for my fragility of heart and that You guard and protect me even when I'm undeserving.

Thank You that You know the way I'll take and will see me through it to the end. I love You and thank You for Your tender mercies, which are evident in the midst of Your sovereign role over all. Help me thank You more frequently as I recognize You as the King of kings and Lord of lords.

Supplication

God, I desire to know You more intimately in this area of Your sovereign role. I desire to see Your hand move mountains and defeat the enemy who raises his ugly head against Your rule.

Show Yourself strong in my life, God, that I may know Your strength and sovereignty all the more. Make my feet walk along the paths that are firm, and rescue me from any dangers the enemy sends my way. I know that in Your sovereign rule, any threat the enemy makes toward me is wiped away in a moment. You reach down to overturn his plans for destruction in my life and in the lives of those who call You King and Savior.

In Jesus' name, I pray this prayer acknowledging Your sovereign rule over all. Amen.

16

Knowing God Through His Goodness

O taste and see that the LORD is good;
how blessed is the man
who takes refuge in Him!

PSALM 34:8

Adoration

Father, You are good. You exist in infinite goodness and love. Your power, grace, and might shine into the world, giving us the light to lead our way.

I look to You as a standard of goodness to guide me in my own choices and decisions. I align my thoughts and actions under Your rule so I will reflect Your goodness. I adore You for revealing to me what I need to do to make Your name great in my spheres of influence.

You are good. You are holy. You are righteous. You are powerful. Your name is the name above all names. Your grace covers all. Receive my praise, my worship, and my adoration as I bow before You in all humility, honoring You and loving You always.

Confession

God, I confess that when placed against the backdrop of Your goodness and holiness, even my attempts at righteousness are as dark as night. I confess that, at times, even my good actions come wrapped in a spirit of ego. I pat my own back for the good things I do or say.

Yet Your goodness is pure. Forgive me, Father, for those times when my pride casts a looming shadow on the good deeds I seek to do in Your name. Forgive me also for those times when I know the right and good thing to do or say and yet I choose not to do that. Show me how to walk in Your forgiveness freely so guilt doesn't plague me and drag me down to a lower level than I am now. Let me know and taste and see Your goodness even in the midst of my failures, mistakes, and sins.

Thanksgiving

Thank You, Father, that Your goodness is a gift raining down on me, watering me with the wealth of Your kindness, Your gentleness, and Your love. And thank You for Your good gifts from above.

Thank You for supplying all I need to eat and live each day. Thank you for giving me all I need for my emotional and mental well-being. Thank You for surrounding me with good fellowship in the presence of Your body of Christ. Thank You for giving me the eyes to discern good from evil so I have the wisdom to choose the right path.

I know You are good, and Your goodness strengthens and enables me to live a life that is pleasing to You in all that I do.

Supplication

Father, I ask that Your goodness reflect more fully through my words and actions as well as in my thoughts. Let me be a better image-bearer of You by aligning my life according to the fruit of Your Spirit—peace, goodness, gentleness, and self-control.

Make me more aware of my own words and actions ahead of time so I will intentionally choose the right path. Show me Your will so I can walk in it. Let Your lovingkindness surround me with wisdom and grace.

In Jesus' name, I pray all of this concerning Your goodness in all things. Amen.

17

Knowing God Through His Wisdom

Oh, the depth of the riches
both of the wisdom and knowledge of God!
How unsearchable are His judgments
and unfathomable His ways!

<small>ROMANS 11:33</small>

Adoration

God, the wisdom that eludes us as finite mortals rests safely and securely in You. You do not have to search for wisdom; You are wisdom. You embody wisdom. You empower wisdom so others can access it. You direct wisdom so I can find it. The depth of the riches both of the wisdom and Your knowledge is beyond my comprehension. So many things don't make sense to me because I can observe them only through my senses.

But wisdom involves so much more than what can be perceived. It involves the inner workings that hold creation together, provide life, and stabilize societies despite Satan's attempts to destabilize and destroy what You have created. Your wisdom is always leaps ahead of what we know, and I praise You for how great Your wisdom truly is.

Confession

Father, I confess easily and quickly to You that, despite my cognizant awareness and understanding that all wisdom rests in You and comes directly from You, I choose to make my own decisions based on what I know far more frequently than I seek You.

I should look to You to guide my large decisions, but I should also look to You to guide the self-management of my emotions. I should look to You and Your wisdom to speak into what I say before I say it and to help me interpret through spiritual insights what other people are saying and what they truly mean. Instead, I lean on my own understanding and then often pay the consequences.

Forgive me for thinking so highly of myself that I neglect to remember that You are the Source of all wisdom—and that You have plainly said You will give that wisdom to anyone who asks You.

Thanksgiving

Holy God, thank You for the brilliance of Your wisdom and Your willingness to share it with anyone who asks. You do not hide wisdom from us; You make it readily available if we but seek You. Your Word is full of wisdom and knowledge. You have placed the Scriptures within our reach so we can gain insight into how to best live our lives for Your glory, others' good, and our own good as well.

Thank You for supplying wisdom so quickly and for Your patience as You see so many make mistakes only to return to You to ask how to reverse them. Your grace is made manifest through Your restraint as You allow each of us the free will to either live according to wisdom or learn through the difficulties of choosing our own way.

Supplication

God, You've made it clear that wisdom is not Yours alone but that You will freely share it with anyone who asks. So I ask You today for wisdom. I ask for direction. I ask for spiritual maturity and all I need to live my life to the fullest. Teach me Your ways and guide me. Lead me in the level path and show me which direction will lead to the greatest spiritual fruit and impact on others. I want to make a difference for the kingdom, but I need Your wisdom to help me discern how to do that.

Help me see beyond what I can see. Help me understand more than I can understand on my own. Reveal to me Your purposes for my life and the highest good in all of the choices placed in front of me each day.

In Jesus' name, I praise You for Your wisdom, and I ask for Your wisdom. Amen.

18

Knowing God Through His Lovingkindness

Your lovingkindness, O LORD,
extends to the heavens,
Your faithfulness reaches to the skies.

PSALM 36:5

Adoration

God, where would I be without Your lovingkindness? How could I navigate through life with all of the ups and downs and twists and turns if I didn't know Your love lies behind every challenge?

Your love undergirds me when I feel as though I've lost my own stability. Your love keeps me filled with hope. I praise You, for Your lovingkindness extends to the heavens and beyond. Your faithfulness reaches to the skies. Your love covers the earth and all of her inhabitants, bringing peace in the midst of chaos and crisis.

I honor You and adore You for Your ability to love completely and compassionately, even when those You love often dismiss You or challenge You. I lift up Your name in praise and adoration, knowing that my life and all of the wonderful things I've been able to experience are a direct result of Your love toward me.

Confession

Father, forgive me for failing to cherish Your love as I should. Forgive me for neglecting to connect the blessings, goodness, and favor in my life directly to Your love. Have mercy on me for the multiple times I've started my day without even acknowledging that Your love kept me safe and alive throughout the night as I slept with nothing to protect me but Your love.

I want to be more aware of Your love, God. And yet I confess that I often overlook it in the simplest of demonstrations, such as Your provision of warmth, oxygen, health, and the ability to think and read and pray. These basic provisions You provide me every moment of every day are an extension of Your love, and I honor You for Your great love and all You have given me that comes from it.

Thanksgiving

Thank You, God, for this great and awesome attribute of Your love—Your lovingkindness. Thank You for the forgiveness given me as a result of Your love. Thank You for the delight supplied to me because of Your love. Thank You for the basic necessities of life as well as the extravagant gifts—both come as an outworking of Your love. Thank You that because You love me, I am able to love You. Thank You that because You have taught me what love is and how it's to be shown, I am able to give love to others that benefits them as well.

Your love sustains me. It's my very life.

Supplication

Father, I want to know Your love even more than I do today; I want to recognize it. Help me spot Your lovingkindness so I don't run the risk of failing to thank You for what You do. Open my eyes to see and recognize what Your love toward me and toward all of humanity looks like.

Let Your love set me free to smile, laugh, hope, and love others more fully. Give me wisdom on how to better function according to the principles of love so I will be a blessing to those who need it most. Make my heart tender so my love will be authentic. Cause me to learn how to better love those You place in my path, including myself. Let lovingkindness define me as I have known it to define You so I will truly reflect You in who I am.

In the name of Jesus, I pray all of these things concerning the greatness of Your lovingkindness. Amen.

19

Knowing God Through His Covenant of Peace

"The mountains may be removed and the hills may shake,
but My lovingkindness will not be removed from you,
and My covenant of peace will not be shaken,"
says the LORD who has compassion on you.

ISAIAH 54:10

Adoration

Holy God, peace is the often-elusive prize we seek in our lives, not real-izing we're seeking it because we forgot what it's like. We chase after other things thinking they are peace, such as significance, accomplish-ment, entertainment, and material goods.

But You alone are peace. You exist in a state of peace. Peace flows from Your veins as the life-giving Spirit of our souls. And You have said a covenant of peace should never be removed from us, those of us who follow You. Even though mountains themselves are removed and hills shake due to the chaos of this world, Your lovingkindness will never be removed. Your covenant of peace will never be shaken. I praise You and honor You, for You have great compassion on those You love.

Confession

Father, forgive me for confusing peace with control—my control. Forgive me for assuming peace is the result of all things going according to my plan and not Yours. Peace doesn't result from me getting my way; peace flows from You as the Source. Your covenant of peace gives life to my spirit and hope to my bones.

Yet I often look for peace and try to force it through manipulating circumstances or people all around me. Or I try to fill my life with pleasures, somehow thinking they translate into peace. But You are peace, and peace is not a prize to be won. It's a gift You have already given if I will just receive it. Forgive me for complicating the process of Your placing the blessing of peace into my life.

Thanksgiving

God, thank You for Your peace. Thank You for not holding it out like a carrot to be earned. You provide a covenant of peace based on Your commitment. Your kingdom is full of peace. Your laws comprise that which produces peace. And Your desire for me is that I live in peace, not only with myself but also with my family and my community—and most importantly, with You.

Thank You that peace can be obtained and enjoyed in this life that brings so much confusion through Satan's attempts to disrupt the love and peace that define You and define all those who follow You. Thank You that peace can be shared with others when we as Your kingdom followers demonstrate what it means to live according to the rules of peace as opposed to the unrighteous rules of selfishness, greed, envy, and war. I love Your peace, and I ask for it to be so prevalent in my life that I know no other way but to walk in the footsteps of peace, no matter what Satan drops in my path.

Supplication

God, I want to know Your peace in my life. I want to experience Your peace in my emotions. I want the peace that passes all understanding to be manifest in my spirit when I need it the most.

I ask for wisdom on how to access and rest in Your peace at a greater level than I have ever experienced. Help me have the willpower and self-restraint to turn away from gossip, fear-mongering, and empty chatter, which lead to unrest. Draw my heart and mind toward Your Word, and let it guide me into a mind-set of perpetual peace.

In the name of Your Son, Jesus Christ, I pray as I honor You, the God who covenants peace with me and with those You love. Amen.

20

Knowing God Through His Preeminence

"I am the Alpha and the Omega,"
says the Lord God,
"who is and who was and
who is to come, the Almighty."

REVELATION 1:8

Adoration

I adore You, heavenly Father. You are the beginning. You are the end. You are all that comes in between. Because of You I have a beginning. Because of You I'm able to be here—to learn, explore, experience, know, and develop. I praise You for this opportunity we call *life*. You have blessed me through Your preeminence.

I worship You and lift up Your name as the great and mighty God You truly are. Lord God, You are, You were, and You are to come. You know no past or future—everything is present to You. You exist in the eternal NOW. I may not be able to understand that because I exist in time. But this reality causes me to worship You all the more as I depend on You to know where I'm going—because You are already there. Your wisdom guides because Your wisdom knows what is to come. What is to come is already known by You.

Confession

Father, I confess that, in my lack of understanding and comprehension of how You transcend this very real element known as "time," I fail to look to You as I should for guidance. I have access to You—the one true God, who is already alive in what I know as the "future." Yet I still choose to go by my own common sense and my own direction rather than seek You and Your guidance throughout my days, weeks, months, and years.

Forgive me for being so shortsighted that I neglect to tap into Your oversight, which exists above all. Thank You for Your patience with me as You seek to expand my thinking to take in the existence of the preeminence that defines You.

Thanksgiving

Thank You for the peace that comes through an awareness of Your preeminence. Thank You for the wisdom in realizing that You are free to give because You have already been in my future and You already know what will come about. I don't need to worry, because You know what is to come, and You have offered to direct me.

Thank You for making Yourself known and knowable to me through Your Word, prayer, meditation, and intimacy with You. Thank You for the times when You directed me away from what would have brought about challenges I didn't need to go through. Thank You that Your grace transcends my limited understanding of who You truly are.

Supplication

Father, help me know You more. Help me know how to know You more fully. Give me insight into what it means to walk according to Your ways. Show me what it's like to let go of the fear of my future or future events because I can rest in the reality of Your love, Your wisdom, and Your all-knowing care.

Guide me according to the path that brings You the greatest glory and brings me the highest good. Show me the steps to take as I walk into Your present, otherwise known as my future. I want my eyes to focus on You because You are already there—leading me and developing me for what I will one day face. Let my decisions and choices reflect a deep, abiding relationship with the God who is preeminent over all, my King.

In Jesus' precious name, I pray all of these things in honor of Your preeminence for all time. Amen.

21

Knowing God Through His Fatherly Love

"I will be a father to you,
and you shall be sons and daughters to Me,"
says the Lord Almighty.

2 CORINTHIANS 6:18

Adoration

God in heaven, You are my loving Father. You care just as a good father cares. You love just as a good father loves. You protect just as a good father protects. You guide just as a good father guides. These are reasons I worship You and love You with my whole heart, my whole mind, and my whole soul.

Each step I take has been carefully thought out by You ahead of time. Should I turn to the left and get off the path of obedience, You have already thought through how to call out to me to draw me back to You. Should I continue on the path of righteousness, You have already gone before me to bless me along the way.

I adore You, for Your love is consistent. Your grace is constant. Your kindness is everlasting. I rest in Your arms, my Father and my God, as I look to You to provide everything I need to pursue my purpose and Your kingdom calling on my life.

Confession

Father, You are near, yet I push You away so very often. You are a caring Father—in fact, You are a perfect Father. And yet I project human frailty and failings onto You in Your role, causing me to doubt You and guard myself from getting too close to You.

Forgive me for at times refusing to look past the earthly definition of a father so I can truly see who You are. Give me the mercy I need to overcome any judgment I have toward this role as father. Help me embrace Your embracing of me in all ways so I can learn what it means to have and experience a perfect, true, and loving Father who looks out for my best interest at all times.

Thanksgiving

Father, thank You for modeling true love to me in such a way that enables me to know You and experience the goodness of Your care. Thank You for not only being the great and awesome God who created all things and is the ruler and King over all things, but for also choosing to relate to me as a loving and intimate Father.

Thank You that Your love knows no bounds. Your redemption doesn't have a limit to which You will go to draw me back to You and Your favor and blessings for my life. You are a consistent Father who showers grace as a natural result of Your simply being You. Thank You that I am invited to know You in this close and personal way.

Supplication

Father, I want to know You more. I want to experience this role and attribute of Yours more. I want to understand what it means to walk through life with You as my good Father.

Whisper in my ear when I'm about to make a wrong choice. Let me know ahead of time when I'm about to say something that's not in alignment with Your perfect will. Encourage me with Your confidence and joy when I'm on the right path or need to speak up about Your truth but lack the courage to do so. Remind me who I am in Christ—that I am whole, strong, stable, and able.

In the name of Jesus Christ, I pray this prayer to You, my good and loving Father. Amen.

22

Knowing God Through His Power and Might

The LORD of hosts has planned, and who can frustrate it?
And as for His stretched-out hand, who can turn it back?

ISAIAH 14:27

Adoration

Lord, You are the God of our fathers. You are God in the heavens. You are the ruler over all the kingdoms of the nations. Power and might are in Your hand, and no one can stand against You. I bring You my honor. I bring You my praise. I bring You my adoration, knowing that all I am is a result of who You are and Your gifts of grace to me.

I bless Your name with my whole heart, trusting in Your unending care and the strength of Your right hand. You deliver me from my enemies. You overpower those who come against me. Your power reaches to the highest heights and stretches across the universe beyond my grasp of understanding.

Show me Your might and give me a fresh view of who You are so I can honor You according to the honor due You.

Confession

Father, fear bubbles up in me when I forget how strong, mighty, and powerful You truly are. I give in to emotions of uncertainty or shame when I fail to take in the totality of Your strength.

Forgive me for allowing my emotions to control my thoughts rather than allowing my thoughts, based on the truth of Your Word, to dictate my emotions. Show me how to rely on the stability of Your strength in such a way that it provides me with clarity and stability of my own. Thank You for Your generous grace and unending mercy in light of my ongoing frailty and forgetfulness of how great You truly are.

Thanksgiving

Thank You, God, for the power of Your hand. Thank You for the assurance of Your might. Thank You for the reminder that I have a mighty King I can run to when things get too difficult for me to bear on my own. When my emotions overwhelm me, I sometimes shut down. But thank You that You provide clarity when I remind myself of Your might and then go to You.

Thank You that I can depend on You when things feel like they're out of control. Thank You that hope is found in Your name and the meaning of life is located in Your presence. You overpower the opposition that seeks to tear me down, whether internally or externally. I praise You for Your might.

Supplication

Father, show me how to better lean on You, to tap into Your strength so that my strength is made complete. Guide me when I rush out on my own without thinking. Remind me to look to You first. I want to know the power of Your might, which works within me. Perfect me in Your presence so that I, too, go through my life with strength.

I am strong in You. You are strong through me. Help me not forget or dismiss that truth. Give me the wisdom to use and access Your strength to its fullest potential in and through me for the greater good of all involved and for Your glory. May I be a part of advancing Your kingdom agenda on earth.

In Jesus' name, I pray this prayer in honor and acknowledgment of Your great power. Amen.

23

Knowing God Through His Thoughts

As the heavens are higher than the earth, so are My ways higher than your ways and My thoughts than your thoughts.

ISAIAH 55:9

Adoration

Father, thank You for Your invaluable wisdom. Thank You for not being limited to the knowledge of men or the methods of humanity. Thank You for providing me with wisdom beyond my own understanding. And thank You that I can trust You to lead me where I need to go.

You are in the heavens, and You rule from a position higher than the earth. Your ways are higher than my ways. Your thoughts are higher than my thoughts. Your understanding stretches beyond what I can even imagine. I adore You, for You transcend the thinking of humanity and provide insight into the inner workings of the universe and all that is. I worship Your great wisdom and lift Your name in praise and awe and endless wonder.

Confession

God, far too often I get lost in my thoughts. I get lost in my understanding. I get stuck in my limited awareness and incomplete ability to fully comprehend the nature and truth of all things. And I confess that even though I know my thoughts aren't as wise or comprehensive as Yours, I still lean on them more. This leads me to draw the wrong conclusions and often waste a lot of time, emotional energy, and strength pursuing that which isn't from You.

Forgive me for lifting the value of my thoughts higher than Yours through my actions. Forgive me for neglecting to go to the Source of all truth for all I do, think, and say. Forgive me for marginalizing the One who knows all, sees all, and is over all.

Thanksgiving

Thank You, Father, for sharing the greatness of Your thoughts with me through Your Word. Thank You for honoring me with wisdom from above. Thank You for making Yourself known to me and for continuing to make Yourself known to me in all things.

Thank You that Your thoughts can overpower my worry, my anxiety, my regret, and my shame. I seek Your truth to make it manifest in my own thinking, Father. Show me how to rely on You more fully—and thank You for giving me the opportunity to do that.

Supplication

Lord, I ask for Your thoughts to overpower mine. I ask that the peace that passes understanding, which comes from You, will be fully alive in me.

Let me know Your thoughts, God. Give me insight into Your wisdom. Show me the path to take. Light my way. Guide me according to what You know so I don't get trapped by what I know. Reveal to me the deep mysteries of the ages. Enlighten my spirit according to Your way. I need Your thoughts to be the prevailing influencer in my life so I don't continue to make wrong choices that lead me into frustration or fear. Give me truth, and let that truth be so dominant that I'm gifted with the grace of rest, peace, and clarity. Let Your Spirit speak Your thoughts not only in my ears but also in my heart so I may please You in all I am.

In Jesus' name, I pray this prayer concerning the powerful depth and wisdom of Your thoughts. Amen.

24

Knowing God Through His Lasting Purposes

*The counsel of the LORD stands forever,
the plans of His heart from generation to generation.*

PSALM 33:11

Adoration

Heavenly Father, Your counsel stands forever. The plans of Your heart last from generation to generation. You are the all-consuming voice that guides, directs, steers, leads, and moves to accomplish Your will according to Your purposes.

I praise You and adore You for the greatness of who You are. I lift up Your name in honor as I realize how solid and unmoving You are from Your own plans. It may look as though humanity has much to say about the nature of life's direction on earth, but ultimately, You have established the plans for all to follow and abide by.

Your name is great and greatly to be praised. Your character is consistent with Your ways. You do not get caught by surprise or make mistakes. I can rest knowing You are ultimately over all. I can rest knowing that Your purposes will stand despite how, each day, the things of life appear everchanging.

Confession

God, even though I understand and realize that Your purposes stand in all that You do and say, I still somehow think my purposes will carry more weight than Yours. I rely on my own thinking, planning, and strategizing rather than going to the Source over all.

Show me how to resist the temptation to look to my own planning rather than rest in Your purposes. I yield and surrender to You, Lord. Forgive me for the arrogance that undergirds a decision to rely heavily on my own purposes and plans rather than on You.

Thanksgiving

Thank You, God, for being so powerful in all that You do. Thank You that, despite knowing Your purposes will stand, You still allow me to take part in the planning and preparation for Your plans to be carried out. You don't have to include me, but You have given me free will to see how I will respond—either by aligning myself under You or choosing my own way.

The lessons I learn are difficult, but I want to thank You for the opportunity to learn them. Each one teaches me I need to trust You all the more, because You know what You are doing and Your purposes will stand throughout all generations.

Supplication

Father, give me the grace to see through my own ego and motives so I can surrender more fully to the purposes You have already created to stand. Humble my heart to such a degree that I can rest in knowing that You have everything under control.

I want to honor You with what I do, but I often get in the way by choosing my will over Your revealed plan. I ask for a greater awareness and discernment between my thoughts and Your purposes so I can choose more wisely from the start. I want to live as a kingdom disciple who carries out Your will for Your glory, for others' good, and for my good as well.

In the loving name of Jesus, I pray all of these things in recognition of how Your plans and purposes will forever stand. Amen.

25

Knowing God Through His Patience

The Lord is not slow about His promise,
as some count slowness, but is patient toward you,
not wishing for any to perish
but for all to come to repentance.

2 Peter 3:9

Adoration

Father, may Your name be glorified and lifted high in praise and adoration. Your character exudes patience. When others respond out of emotion, You are restrained. You withhold wrath as You seek for all to have the opportunity to come to repentance.

I praise You because I know I can rest in Your loving care. I know You will see me through when life becomes difficult. When my emotions lead me down the wrong path, Your patience stays steady to draw me back to You. I give You glory, for Your grace is unending, and Your care covers all.

Confession

Holy God, show me how to better rest in the reality of Your patience. Make me know the depths of Your love so I won't continue in a cycle of despair. I want to have confidence knowing that You alone are the One to whom I must look for my validation and purpose in life, but I confess that I often look to others who aren't nearly as patient as You. When judgments from myself or others crash down on me, I forget to find my significance in my identity as a child of the King.

Thank You for forgiving me and giving me the mercy that comes from the depths of Your love.

Thanksgiving

Lord, thank You for Your never-ending patience. Thank You for drawing me near to You patiently and with kindness. Thank You for helping me be aware of how much patience You have toward me so I don't take it lightly.

Thank You also for teaching me how to be more patient with others and with myself as I follow Your example. Show me what I can do to develop a greater level of patience that will honor You well. So I won't speak my mind abruptly, give me insight into why it's best to refrain from saying everything I think. I want my patience to grow as I experience Your patience toward me.

Supplication

Heavenly Father, make me know Your ways according to Your good pleasure so I can live in a manner that's pleasing to You.

Give me the patience of Job, Lord. Let me look upon life with an objective awareness that gives me the freedom to discern. As You grow and develop my patience, I pray You will also lift me into greater positions of influence over others so I can model this patience to them as well. Equip us all in Your collective body with what we need to show greater patience to one another in the grace of Christ.

In Jesus' holy name, I worship and praise You as I pray this prayer in gratitude for Your loving patience. Amen.

26

Knowing God Through His Graciousness

The LORD is gracious and merciful;
slow to anger and great in lovingkindness.

PSALM 145:8

Adoration

Father, You are full of overwhelming grace. You are both gracious and merciful. I praise Your name, for You are slow to anger and great in lovingkindness. I worship and adore You, for Your love is over all. Your graciousness gives me courage each day to seek new ways to please You.

Your mercy allows me to experience the fullness of my kingdom purpose on earth. You are high and lifted up in the heavenlies and filled with the mercy of the ages. Your mercy and graciousness rain down on those who look to You for provision, life, and hope. When life gets tough and trials compound one upon the other, I look to Your hand of graciousness and benevolence, seeking You above all else. Your holiness shines like light in the darkness.

Confession

Heavenly Lord, make me more aware of my need for Your graciousness so I don't wind up taking it for granted. Forgive me for walking into Your throne room with a spirit of entitlement as if Your mercy and grace are mine because I deserve them. But I've done nothing to deserve Your hand of grace on my life. Your gifts of blessings abound, and yet I have only dismissed You far too often in my own heart or taken credit for things You Yourself have brought about.

Forgive the audacity I've shown You, especially in the areas of Your mercy and graciousness ever apparent in my daily activities, work, and relationships.

Thanksgiving

Father, thank You for Your abundant provision of graciousness to me. Thank You for showing me how to access Your grace through prayer. Thank You for opening my eyes to see Your hand of grace more clearly and for enabling me to honor You in return with the thanksgiving of my heart.

Increase the hope I have for a brighter tomorrow, knowing that Your graciousness is rooted in Your character and consistent with Your attributes. Give me a greater confidence in Your grace, Lord. I look to You with thanksgiving, fully aware that the goodness I experience is a direct result of Your unhindered love and care.

Supplication

God, I want to know Your love more fully through a greater experience of Your graciousness. Open my heart so I'll be able to allow in a deeper level of Your grace and mercy. Awaken my spirit to Your Spirit's presence and to the gifts brought by Your Spirit, such as greater clarity, discernment, and love.

I want to be gracious like You, God. I want to refrain from anger, judgment, and criticism of others as I look to You for Your leading. Show me how to be more like You in how I extend graciousness through what I do and say to others but also to myself.

I love you, God. And in the gracious name of the Lord Jesus Christ, I pray all these things concerning Your graciousness. Amen.

27

Knowing God Through His Encouragement

*May the God who gives perseverance and encouragement
grant you to be of the same mind with one another
according to Christ Jesus.*

ROMANS 15:5

Adoration

Father, You are the One who gives perseverance and encouragement to all. You are the greatest of encouragers. Your love lifts up the hopeless and sparks light where darkness once overshadowed all. Encouragement is at the core of who You are. Life and love spring eternal from You. I worship and praise You, for You are a God who saves the broken and mends the worn.

Today I lift up Your name in praise because of the goodness that spreads from You to all who look to You for life and hope. Let the hope of all humanity find its source in You. Then may we replicate Your love through the encouragement we give to one another. We will praise You through our own acts of kindness. We will honor You as we show perseverance to one another on a greater level than ever before. We will give You the adoration due You by lifting the broken from the depths of despair so they can also find their hope in You, the great Encourager over all.

Confession

Father, I want to know how to become a better encourager, to be more like You. I confess that I often jump to blame or criticism rather than to encouragement. Or I look for someone to encourage me rather than recognizing my role as an encourager to others.

Forgive me for the selfishness that keeps me from encouraging others as I should. David even encouraged himself when he was feeling down or depressed. Forgive me for far too often complaining when life becomes challenging rather than looking to encourage myself with Your Word and a steadfast hope in You. Mold me into a greater encourager for myself as well as for the benefit of others and Your glory, Lord.

Thanksgiving

Holy God, thank You for Your constant encouragement through the powerful truths found in Your Word. Thank You for renewing my spirit with hope and joy, especially when I'm feeling down. Thank You that Your Word reminds me of who I am in You—that I'm a conqueror, victorious—and that I have all I need to fully live out my purpose and destiny.

Thank You for the strength You supply through Your encouragement. You cause me to run and not grow weary. You are the wind beneath my wings. I look to You when I'm worn out and discouraged, and You give me hope. Thank You for continually supplying all I need as life to my spirit and hope to my soul.

Supplication

Lord, I ask that You help me hear You more fully, especially when I feel discouraged. I don't want to become lost in despair to such a degree that I neglect to listen to You. Your encouragement can go only so far if it falls on deaf ears. If I don't hear You, I won't be able to apply Your encouragement to my spirit so I can experience the life You give.

Show me what I need to do to hear You more clearly, Lord. Help me tune out the negative and criticizing voices that seek to gain my attention over Yours.

In Jesus' precious name, I pray this prayer out of a heart of honor for who You are. Amen.

Knowing God Through His Ability to Become Wearied

You have wearied the LORD with your words.
Yet you say, "How have we wearied Him?"
In that you say, "Everyone who does evil is good
in the sight of the LORD, and He delights in them,"
or, "Where is the God of justice?"

MALACHI 2:17

Adoration

Holy God, You are patient. You persevere. You are kind. You are holy. Your compassionate love covers me. And yet You are also just. You are also righteous. And so You become weary of evildoing. You become tired when my words are empty and when my heart is far away. You are not just a stoic being with no emotion. Rather, You care so deeply that it offends You when I keep on sinning in light of Your overarching grace.

Lord, I worship You as I fear You, in honor of who You truly are. I'm grateful that You allow me to see this side of You, not only the side that's giving, kind, and forgiving. I need to know all of You in order to give You the authentic praise due Your name and to rightly reflect Your character with the spirit of my worship of You.

Confession

Holy God, I confess that I don't consider how I've wearied You as often as I should. I confess that I depend on the kindness of Your character to such a large degree that it borders on a spirit of entitlement.

I ask You to forgive me even in the midst of Your being wearied by my sin and my propensity to dismiss You in the face of difficulties I think I can solve. Rather than look for ways You can see me through challenging circumstances, I often seek to maneuver my own ways outside of Your will. Please have mercy on me and correct me, Lord. But do so with mercy, or I will not be able to stand beneath the weight of Your just hand.

Thanksgiving

Lord, thank You for reminding me of the importance of fearing You through a reverent awareness of Your holiness. Thank You for letting me see glimpses of Your greatness so I can rightfully honor You in my thoughts, with my words, and through my actions. Thank You that even though You are wearied by my sin, You embrace me with Your love.

Thank You for showing great mercy in the midst of being wearied by the world and its inhabitants. You have extended Your patience in light of Your disdain of the evil that takes place. I ask You, Lord, for an increased acknowledgment in my life and in our culture for Your patience and an increased awareness of how we've wearied the great God who rules over all.

Supplication

Father, I don't want to weary You with my sins. I don't want to try Your patience. I want to please You in all I do. Help me live more according to the law of Love You have given to us as a way of honoring You in all we do. Help me love You with all my heart, all my soul, all my spirit, and all my strength.

Help me also love others as I love myself. When I live my life and make my decisions by these two principles of love, I will not weary You; I will honor You. Show me what it means to bring You delight, Lord, and cause me to focus more fully on what brings You joy rather than on what causes You to sigh.

All in the name of Jesus, I pray this prayer with a heart of gratitude. Amen.

29

Knowing God Through His Direction

May the Lord direct your hearts into the love of God and into the steadfastness of Christ.

2 Thessalonians 3:5

Adoration

Holy God, You always provide a light to direct me to and guide me on the path You know is the best one for me to take. I lift Your name in praise knowing I can depend on You to show the way. I honor You, for Your wisdom stretches into the future to guide and direct according to the best possible outcome for all. I love You, God, and I want to know how to follow You better.

Let the glory due You overshadow the doubts that plague the hearts of humanity. Break through to show us the way toward life, peace, and love. May You receive the praise You deserve and bask in the love that is Yours as You guide us in the ways we should go.

Confession

Father, You know the way I am to go, which will lead me to fulfill the purpose You have established for me on earth. You know the path I should take and the decisions I should make that will enable me to live out my destiny. And yet, even though I know this about You, I often choose my own way and my own leading over Yours.

Forgive me for this shortsightedness, which limits my own potential. Forgive me for the pride that wells up within me, causing me to think I may even know better than You rather than truly seek Your guidance and direction each step of the way.

Thanksgiving

Lord, thank You for guiding me with patience, understanding, peace, and love. Thank You for guiding me with wisdom and kindness. You do not guide me into the dangerous aspects of life unless You have a purpose for me to learn in those experiences. You do not guide me toward pointless activities or endless pursuits that add up to meaninglessness. Rather, You guide me toward that which produces spiritual growth and development, and I thank You. You guide me toward that which produces life and hope.

Thank You for the wisdom of Your direction and for making me aware of how to access Your guidance through Your loving Word.

Supplication

Loving God, I ask for Your guidance on the specific aspects of my life. I realize when I need to ask You to guide me for major decisions, but far too often I leave You out of the planning of daily activities or even out of my conversations with others.

I want You to guide me on what to say so my words are ministers of grace seasoned with love to those who hear them. I want You to guide me on how to spend my time each day so I'm using it wisely to advance Your kingdom and develop my own spiritual maturity. I ask You to guide me on large choices and small, and even on what I engage for entertainment.

Guide all aspects of my life, Lord. Teach me how to hear Your guidance more clearly and yield to Your leading.

In the powerful name of Jesus Christ, I pray all these things concerning Your gift of direction. Amen.

30

Knowing God Through His All-Knowingness

Remember the former things long past,
for I am God, and there is no other;
I am God, and there is no one like Me,
declaring the end from the beginning,
and from ancient times things which have not been done,
saying, "My purpose will be established,
and I will accomplish all My good pleasure."

ISAIAH 46:9-10

Adoration

Lord, so much of life is unknown. I can see only bits and pieces. Uncertainties and confusions lurk around decisions, which at times make it difficult to know what to do and think. People offer their opinions, but they're not You. Only You know all things to know. You are God. There is no other. No one like You exists.

You declare the end from the beginning. You know the future before we get there. What You say will happen does happen. From ancient times to present times, You know all. Your purpose will be established, and You will accomplish all of Your good pleasure. I praise and worship You, for You are truly holy, loving, and all-knowing in every way.

Confession

Father, I can see only what is in front of me, and even then it's foggy. As Paul said, we can only see through a mirror dimly at this point. Things are not entirely clear. And yet knowing that You are all-knowing and that I have only a limited view, I still rely on my own decision-making skills rather than look to You to lead, guide, assure, and correct me— and to give me peace.

Forgive me for failing to follow You or for even failing to study the revelations made clear in Your Word. These acts of disobedience to You only cause me trouble. Forgive me for not looking to Your leading and guidance for answers I desire to have.

Thanksgiving

Holy God, thank You that the breadth and the depth of Your knowledge spans all there is to know. Thank You that I can know You, the One who knows all. Thank You that You have made Yourself available to me to be known, and that in knowing You, I can tap into all wisdom, all knowledge, and all love.

Thank You for being my guide and my Source of all things, and for giving me the ability to discern between truth and lies. Thank You that You keep all things in order. Thank You for supplying all we need on this planet for it to function and for life to continue and move forward. It's all held together by Your knowledge and Your never-ending care and love.

Supplication

God, I want to know You more fully. I want to search Your mind and know Your thoughts. I ask to know the truth. I ask to have great discernment to understand what You know. I want to know what You know in such a way that it impacts my emotions, my thoughts, my words, and my actions. I want to know the hope that comes in resting in full confidence of Your knowledge.

Lord, show me how I can tap into Your all-knowingness at a greater level. How can I gain greater insight into Your Word? Let Your Holy Spirit guide me to Scripture that reveals what I need to know when I need to know it. Give me strength to resist the temptation to turn to those who don't know all as my Source for understanding. Help me to instead look to You always for a greater understanding of all things.

In Jesus' name, I pray this prayer in praise of Your knowing all things. Amen.

Knowing God Through His Omniscience

*"Can a man hide himself in hiding places
so I do not see him?" declares the LORD.
"Do I not fill the heavens and the earth?"
declares the LORD.*

JEREMIAH 23:24

Adoration

God, there is no hiding from You. There is nowhere I can go that's outside of Your ability to find me. When I feel lost, it's only because I've lost sight of my way, not because You have lost sight of me. That's not possible. You always know where I am, and You can reach in to redeem me from the wrong path I've taken.

I take comfort in knowing that You know all. You are omniscient and everywhere at all times. If You were not, this world would quickly unravel, and we would all be in an irreversible mess. I praise You, for Your omniscience brings about our security. I worship and adore You because Your omniscience gives me comfort in knowing that I don't need to fear what I can't see or what the enemy is using to attack me. You see all. You know all. And You defend Your own according to Your great will and Your perfect plan.

Confession

Lord, I can see only what I can see, and I can be only where I am. I'm limited to the skin You have placed my soul within. And as a result, I sometimes forget that You are greater than all I know. I often rely on my own limited sight and limited understanding rather than tap into the awareness of all through my personal connection to You.

Forgive me for dismissing the wonder of who You truly are by insisting on making plans according to only what I know and comprehend. Forgive me for not giving You the glory, praise, adoration, and trust due You as the omniscient God You are. I confess that I don't honor You as I should, and for that I ask for Your forgiveness, Your mercy, and Your compassion.

Thanksgiving

Thank You, God, for the greatness of who You are. Thank You for all You know and Your ability to be in all locations at all times. Thank You that Your omniscience allows me to let go of worry, fear, and anxiety as I learn to trust in You more fully. Thank You for making it a point to let humanity know about Your omniscience so we can gain a greater understanding of Your kingdom rule.

You sit rightfully above all and are able to guide and direct all due to Your omniscience. Thank You for revealing Yourself in this way to me so I can better know You according to the reality of Your reign, Your rule, and Your righteous, omniscient ways.

Supplication

Holy God, help me rest more fully in the truth of Your powerfully expansive omniscience. Help me take heart in knowing that You know all and see all. Help this truth give me a sense of comfort in all I do so I won't fear what lurks around every corner, because You are already there.

I also want to know more of what You know. Help me grow more closely to You so I can gain insight into what I can't know on my own because of my limited perceptions. Cultivate my spiritual sensitivities so I can know and love and abide with You more intimately as the great omniscient God over all.

In Jesus' matchless name, I pray this prayer in praise of Your omniscience. Amen.

32

Knowing God Through His Immutability

I, the Lord, *do not change; therefore you,*
O sons of Jacob, are not consumed.

Malachi 3:6

Adoration

Father, so much has changed and continues to change in our world. What seems like normal morphs into a new normal before our eyes. What we're told one day is contradicted the next, or so it seems. Yet one thing remains the same: Despite all the changes we go through on earth and with one another, You remain unchanged. Your immutability means You are a God who changes not. I praise You and worship You for Your changelessness in the ever-changing continuum we call life.

Let people see Your stable ways, Lord, so we can all praise You and seek Your security in all that we do. Let us as a church body worship You more fully and frequently for the constancy that is truly who You are.

Confession

Lord, I confess that change can frighten me. Too many changes carried out too quickly can leave me feeling anxiety and dread. When I don't know what to expect or what lurks around the next corner, my emotions sometimes get the best of me.

I confess that I haven't come to know Your immutability as deeply and intimately as I should. Forgive me for looking at my circumstances or the circumstances of our world more than I look at You. In You I will find peace, security, strength, and assurance. Your immutability is the blessed assurance my soul seeks.

Thanksgiving

Heavenly Father, thank You for Your dependability. Thank You for always being stable. Thank You that, even though society sometimes looks as if it's on the precipice of crumbling before our very eyes, You are calm, assured, and unchanging.

Nothing catches You off guard. I consider that pandemics can spread around the globe, but You are not taken by surprise. You know what will happen, and You are ever-present to provide guidance and wisdom as we navigate the onset of such times. Thank You for Your loving care, which is the same yesterday, today, and forever.

Supplication

Holy God, I want to be more solidly like You in what I feel and in my actions. I don't want to allow my emotions to dictate my choices. I want Your Word to take root so deeply within me that I, too, am stable and unchanging despite what life puts on my plate.

I ask for this intimacy, which will produce a greater inner peace and stability for me. I ask to know You more and to love You more completely. Help me understand the importance of understanding that my identity comes tied to You and the assuring love You give. When I do, then I can rest in Your unchanging love, peace, and provision.

In the incomparable name of Jesus Christ, I pray this prayer in honor of Your unchanging nature. Amen.

33

Knowing God Through His Justice

The Rock! His work is perfect, for all His ways are just;
a God of faithfulness and without injustice,
righteous and upright is He.

DEUTERONOMY 32:4

Adoration

Father, You are just. You are the Rock. Your work is perfect, and all Your ways are just. You are a God of faithfulness, and You are without injustice. Righteousness defines who You are. You are upright and full of love. When we're to look for a model of justice, we're to focus our eyes on You. I bless Your holy name and lift Your name in worship and praise. Let Your name be lifted up and highly exalted over all. I give You the honor due Your name.

Show me how I can better adore You and worship You when it comes to this area of Your justice. Often, I feel as if I should hide from Your justice because I know what I've done against You. But, Lord, because of the mercies of Jesus Christ, You do not want me to hide. I can come boldly to You, fully forgiven and trusting that Your grace will meet me with love. I praise You for the freedom I have in Jesus Christ.

Confession

Father, I confess my quick rush to a call for justice when it comes to those I feel have harmed me, and I ask for Your forgiveness. I hope and pray that You will enable me to show the kind of grace You have shown to me. When I look for You to hand down swift justice, I'm forgetting the many times I've cried out to You for Your great mercy. Forgive me for my impatience when it comes to others. And forgive me for failing to fully honor You for the patience You show me when it comes to giving me mercy rather than the justice I deserve.

I know You are perfect and that all Your ways are just. I want to walk according to Your perfect plan in all things and live a life that models and reflects the justness of who You are.

Thanksgiving

Thank You, God, that You truly are just. You do not have one standard one day and another standard on another day. Your justice isn't a moving target, making us unable to identify it and aim.

I give thanks to You knowing I can rest in Your overarching care as You seek to maintain a just rule over all. Thank You for making Your ways clear and that we don't have to guess what You expect of us. Your heart reflects Your perfection and Your justice in all things. I thank You for allowing me to get to know You more fully as I've experienced Your justice coupled with Your great mercy.

Supplication

Heavenly Lord, I want to know Your perfection and righteousness on a greater level. I want to understand the way You lead and love. So I can show greater love to myself and to those around me, give me a greater glimpse into what Your justice looks like and how You keep it coupled with Your mercy. Let me honor You more completely through choices that align under Your overarching and comprehensive rule.

I love You, and I ask that my love for You will only deepen and grow as I come to know You in a more intimate way.

In Christ's name, I pray all these things concerning Your justice. Amen.

Knowing God Through His Heart to Revive and Restore

Thus says the high and exalted One who lives forever,
whose name is Holy, "I dwell on a high and holy place,
and also with the contrite and lowly of spirit
in order to revive the spirit of the lowly
and to revive the heart of the contrite."

ISAIAH 57:15

Adoration

Father, I worship You, for You are high and exalted. You are the One who has always lived, and You will remain forever. You are before all things and after all things as well.

I know You are holy because Your character reveals Your perfect ways. You love with a pure love that includes grace, patience, kindness, and tender care. You dwell in a high and holy place. You are worthy of all wonder and awe. Yet You also dwell with the contrite and lowly in spirit in order to give Your strength to those who need it most. You are high yet also accessible to all.

God, I worship You for Your willingness and ability to revive the spirit of the lowly and to restore the heart of the contrite.

Confession

Heavenly Lord, forgive me for my lack of awe when it comes to Your great ways. Forgive me for seeking alternate distractions or approaches to overcoming any pain I face rather than looking to You in wonder and receiving Your love. You are there to fully revive and restore my spirit when I need You most, but I often go to You last.

God, I ask that You show me patience and gently remind me to come to You when I'm feeling down or depressed. Lead me away from temptation so I don't seek to alleviate any suffering or challenges I face through illicit ways. Rather, help me have confidence in seeking You as I approach Your throne of grace.

Thanksgiving

God, thank You for Your heart that seeks to heal. Thank You for the kindness and compassion of who You truly are. Thank You that I know I can trust You to listen to me when I'm hurting and that I can trust that You will be there for me when no one else seems to be. Thank You that You hear the prayers I pray, even the ones I don't fully voice. Rather, Your Spirit interprets my groaning to You in such a way that opens the windows of heaven so that Your loving heart can revive and restore me.

Thank You that You are over all, that You see all, and that You care for all.

Supplication

God, I want to know Your comforting care on a regular basis. I ask You to revive my spirit where it has become jaded or shut down. Reach into my heart and restore the passion and love that once grew there so well but have become dormant over time and through difficulties. Revive me, God, with a heart that seeks after You to know You fully and with great enthusiasm. Restore me with a willing spirit that I might do Your works and will in my life, not out of compulsion but because of pure joy and love.

Will You guide me into a greater intimacy with You, God, so that I can know and experience the full healing strength of Your love?

In Jesus' name, I pray this prayer, asking to more closely know Your heart of restoring care. Amen.

35

Knowing God Through His Truth

Sanctify them in the truth; Your word is truth.

JOHN 17:17

Adoration

Father, You are truth. In our day, people think truth has many versions. Yet there is only one truth—and You are this truth. Truth can't be modified. Truth doesn't adjust to the current cultural climate or norms. Truth is rooted and founded in You.

Knowing You means knowing the truth. Knowing You means knowing the way I'm to go. Knowing You means understanding how to apply wisdom to all of life's choices. I praise You because You have made truth available to me through Your life and through the character of Your overarching truth. Your Word is truth, and I'm sanctified when I surrender to Your truth and honor You in all I do.

Confession

Heavenly Lord, forgive me when I look for information outside of Your truth and fail to examine Your Word. I confess that I often seek answers to what I'm thinking or feeling from other sources outside of You. You are the truth, and yet I look to other things or people to inform my decisions.

This must hurt Your heart, and I'm sorry for that. Forgive me. I ask Your forgiveness for downplaying Your character, that You embody all truth. I downplay this by seeking other people's opinions or even by choosing my own opinion over what You know is the best thing for me to do or think. I ask for Your grace and mercy in helping me to see the misinformation I believe to be true. Help me to discern more fully.

Thanksgiving

God, thank You for giving me the Truth through Your own existence and the revelation of Your Word. Thank You for giving me the opportunity to be sanctified by Your truth. Thank You for the patience You show me when I turn from truth and pursue my own beliefs. You give me great patience as I examine various thoughts. Thank You for the restraint You show when I seek other sources of direction outside of You, all the while gently pulling me back to Your Word and Your truth. As John 1:17 says, "The Law was given through Moses; grace and truth were realized through Jesus Christ."

Thank You for the grace and truth You have made available to me through Jesus Christ so that I may live out my destiny in Your kingdom plan.

Supplication

Holy Father, not only are You the Source of all truth, but You have given me access to You through Your Word. You are truth. Your Word is truth. I need look no further than You to know all I need to know to guide, direct, and lead me. Because of You I can be sanctified.

I pray I will abide more closely with You in Your truth. I pray I will come to know Your truth deep within so I'm not drawn away into double-mindedness. Shine the light of Your truth upon my soul, and chase the darkness of deception from my thoughts, my heart, and my spirit. Show me the power I have when I function according to Your truth. Let me be a light that shows what it means to live and prosper in Your truth so others will want to do the same.

In the name of Jesus, I pray this prayer concerning the reality and assurance of Your truth. Amen.

36

Knowing God Through His Role as Entry to the Kingdom

Jesus answered and said to him,
"Truly, truly, I say to you,
unless one is born again he
cannot see the kingdom of God."

JOHN 3:3

Adoration

Father, Your kingdom covers all. Your kingdom agenda is Your comprehensive rule over all. Nothing of worth or value sits outside of Your kingdom. It's the summation of all that matters, all that is, and all that will go on throughout time and eternity.

Yet the only entry point into Your kingdom is through You as well. You have made the way for humanity to enter into the divine blessings of Your covenantal care as manifested in Your kingdom rule. We come through salvation based on faith alone in Christ alone. I worship and adore You for providing the pathway into Your kingdom to anyone who chooses You. You have made the way clear. The gospel is available to all.

May Your name and the name of our Lord and Savior, our righteous King, Jesus, be praised always for who You truly are and all You have done for us who seek You.

Confession

Holy Lord, You have made the way for all to be saved and enter into Your kingdom. You have provided the path, and yet we often overlook the importance of this entry into Your kingdom and all Your kingdom supplies, such as eternal salvation and the preservation of the soul. I know I do.

Forgive me for failing to share with others this good news of Your eternal salvation and entry into the kingdom through Jesus Christ. Forgive me for my lack of taking this seriously through the honor and reverence of my heart or as a regular part of my prayers to You. I ask for Your forgiveness and compassionate care so I can be fully motivated to follow Your kingdom rule in all I do. I want to share about Your path of salvation to more people in any way I can. I want to take this role more seriously, so I start by asking for Your forgiveness for those times when I do not.

Thanksgiving

Thank You, Father, for the entry into the kingdom that comes to me through something You did, something I would be wholly unable to do. Thank You for providing the way for sinful humanity to reign and rule under Your rule as the sinless God. Thank You for allowing me to be born into a culture and time when I could learn about You and come to know Jesus Christ as my Lord and Savior. Thank You that I'm able to pray openly to You with prayers of gratitude and thanksgiving.

Thank You for all of my loved ones who know You as well. Thank You that we can one day share the gift of eternity in Your great eternal kingdom with You. I also pray for a greater burden on my heart to pray for those loved ones and friends who don't yet know You or have not yet trusted in Jesus for their salvation. I thank You for the work You are doing in their lives as You continue to draw them to You.

Supplication

Jesus, You are the entry into the kingdom. You provide the path for eternal salvation through the ultimate sacrifice You made on the cross. Help me treasure Your gift of salvation and all that You did to supply it to me. Help me think on this more than I do. I want to honor You in my heart and with my thoughts, so I ask You to make my spirit tender toward You, Jesus.

As I get to know You and the power of Your salvation, I will come to know God, the Father, because You are the exact representation of Him—and because through Your Spirit, He is revealed to me. Help me know the joy of Your suffering and the power of Your resurrection that allow me to experience all the benefits and blessings of the kingdom now that I have entered into this new covenant with God Himself.

In the precious name of Jesus Christ, I pray all of these things concerning Your role as entry into the kingdom. Amen.

Knowing God Through Knowing What Delights Him

Thus says the LORD,
"Let not a wise man boast of his wisdom,
and let not the mighty man boast of his might,
let not a rich man boast of his riches;
but let him who boasts boast of this,
that he understands and knows Me,
that I am the LORD who exercises lovingkindness,
justice and righteousness on earth;
for I delight in these things,"
declares the LORD.

JEREMIAH 9:23-24

Adoration

Father, I worship You in order to bring You joy. You are a God who delights in the praise and adoration of those whom You love. In Your Word, You have told us on what we are to focus. You have made it known to us that a wise person should not boast in their wisdom. A strong person ought not to boast in their strength. A rich person should not count their riches as the basis for their identity and worth. You have said that, instead, we should boast about understanding and knowing You.

My heart's joy resonates in knowing that You, Lord, are the God who exercises lovingkindness, justice, and righteousness on earth. You delight in doing these things on behalf of humanity, and I praise You for Your loving hand.

Confession

Lord, I learned in Your Word how much You love to bring about lovingkindness, justice, and righteousness. You delight in seeing these three brought to light and lives transformed.

Yet the evil in this world does the opposite. Injustice is rampant on many fronts. Unrighteousness flourishes through our films and our music. Apathy and bullying have replaced kindness for many people. I confess to You that I sometimes confuse what I see in the culture with who You are. But You have given us free will as people, and the evil we experience is a result of our own choices, not Your character. Forgive me for ever blaming You for all that is wrong in the world today.

Thanksgiving

God, thank You for being a constant Source of love, hope, and peace. Thank You for ensuring that justice does prevail in the end. We may not always see it now, and I may not always experience kindness at the hands of those I know, but You are a God who sees all. You know all. And You will turn the tide when I look to Your hand to do so.

I thank You that I can call on You in times of trouble and despair. Thank You for modeling to me and to all of us in the body of Christ what it means to take delight in justice, righteousness, and kindness.

Supplication

God, bless me with a greater experience of Your lovingkindness. Let my heart overflow with the hope that comes in knowing You through Your attributes of love. Protect me from my own tendencies toward selfishness or unrighteousness. I want to live my life as a reflection of who You are. Help me to know You more closely in such a way that Your attributes of love, justice, and holiness shine through me to others.

Make me know what it means to delight in doing good things from a good heart, even more so than seeking selfish indulgences from time to time. I want to delight in righteous living as You delight in righteousness on all levels and at all times.

In the name of Jesus Christ, I pray this prayer, asking to more completely know what delights You so I can know You more. Amen.

38

Knowing God Through the Holy Spirit

To us God revealed them through the Spirit;
for the Spirit searches all things, even the depths of God.

1 Corinthians 2:10

Adoration

Lord God, You have provided the way for me to get to know You as much as I possibly want to do so—through the revelation of the Holy Spirit. You have given me access to the revelation of all things through Your Spirit. The Holy Spirit searches all things, even the depths of Your being. The Holy Spirit knows You inside and out and understands Your heart, Your motives, Your desires, and more.

I worship You for the power You have given me through this unique access into who You truly are. I love You and give You praise because Your revelation of truth and love through the Spirit enables me to remain calm in a crisis and tap into the clarity that comes through knowing You. Receive my praise as I give it to You with a full heart.

Confession

My God in heaven, blessed is Your name and holy are You seated high and exalted above all. You expand beyond all that I know and comprehend. You are before time, and You are not bound by time the way I am. The universe rests in the palm of Your mighty hand as a droplet of water in the morning dew.

Yet even though You are so large and magnificent, You have given me access to know You personally. I confess that I sometimes take that access for granted. Forgive me for those moments when I'm dismissive as to the magnitude of Your gift of knowing You through the Holy Spirit.

Thanksgiving

Lord, thank You for the Holy Spirit, who teaches me all things and leads me through all things. Thank You for the Spirit of righteousness, who gives me the opportunity to know You and experience You at a greater level. Make my heart swell to overflowing with the gratitude that comes in truly comprehending what You have given me through this gift of the Holy Spirit. I want to give You the thanksgiving You deserve as You come near to me through this access point of the Spirit.

I also thank You for the insight, truths, and revelation You have made known to me through the wonderful and mighty Holy Spirit.

Supplication

Holy Father, I ask to know You—Your thoughts, Your hopes, Your plans, and Your will. I want to know what is considered the very depths of who You are. Show me greater insights into who You are. Let my spirit commune openly and freely with the Holy Spirit so I can gain the greatest knowledge of You. Make me understand Your Word on a greater level. Cause me to grow as I come to know You more so that my emotions don't dictate my thoughts or actions but I'm ruled by the strength of the wisdom ruling in me.

In Jesus' name, I pray this prayer with a desire to know You more fully through the gracious gift of Your Spirit. Amen.

39

Knowing God Through His Creation

Since the creation of the world His invisible attributes,
His eternal power and divine nature, have been clearly seen,
being understood through what has been made,
so that they are without excuse.

ROMANS 1:20

Adoration

God, I feel Your presence in the midst of Your creation. For since the beginning of time, Your invisible attributes and Your eternal power have been felt and known through Your creation. Your divine nature becomes manifested to us to witness and worship through the handiwork of what You have made. My eyes look upon all of the greatness of Your creative prowess and genius, and my heart responds with awe.

I praise and adore You for the vastness of what You have made. The beauty and intricacy of each element of Your creation speaks to the wisdom of Your heart. Receive my praise and worship as I bow before You in humility and wonder at the works of Your matchless hands.

Confession

Father, the creation You made supplies and sustains every aspect of life. Each atom and molecule contributes to the overall wholeness of who we are and what we're able to do on earth. You have missed nothing needed in creation. You made it all available to us so we don't lack food, air, nutrients, love, and life itself. Your replicating model of life continues to give and to give.

Forgive me for taking all of this for granted in those times when I do. Forgive me for failing to marvel at the majesty of Your bountiful brilliance displayed through Your creation.

Thanksgiving

God, thank You for all of the glimpses I receive of who You are and how deep You are when I observe the miraculous nature of Your creation. My mind can't even fathom all that it takes to have everything functioning without fail.

Thank You for Your sustaining life You have given us through Your creation. Thank You for revealing a bit of Your power, Your grace, Your joy, and Your peace through the beauty of Your creation. Thank You for giving me eyes to see the flowers and the mountains and the wildlife. Thank You for making Yourself known to me through this unique gift of Your creation.

Supplication

I want to know Your creative power more and more each day. I want to know why You chose to create what You did. Do You enjoy Your creation as much as we do? Do You delight in a sunset or watching the waves roll up on the shore? What is Your favorite part of Your creation, God? My heart longs to know the answers to these questions so I can know You all the more.

Show me how to see You more clearly through the revelation of Your creation. Show me how I can take part in helping Your creation to flourish more fully. Let us as a people preserve Your creation, as You have given it to us to cultivate and depend on. I want to feel Your love in my heart when I see the beauty of Your creation, and I ask for more opportunities to experience You more through Your creation.

In Christ's name, I pray this prayer with awe, asking to know You more fully through Your creation. Amen.

40

Knowing God Through His Ability to Strengthen

By smooth words he will turn to godlessness
those who act wickedly toward the covenant,
but the people who know their God will
display strength and take action.

DANIEL 11:32

Adoration

Father, evil lurks in our land and throughout the world. It lurks in hearts, in minds, and in communities. I look to You in prayer and adoration for the strength only You can provide when so much devastation takes place around us. Show Yourself strong in the lives of those who seek You, and let my praise and worship draw Your might into my spirit. I honor You for who You are and for Your strength that goes out to all of us who seek You, God. I lift up Your name as I seek Your strength as my own.

Let Your name be great among the nations. Let Your name be great among the world. Let us see Your mighty hand bring about the peace our hearts seek and desire as You display strength through us to advance Your kingdom agenda on earth.

Confession

Holy God, I confess to You my sins of fear, worry, anxiety, dread—and at times, the inability to move wisely from a standpoint of strength. I confess that when troubles seem to overwhelm me, I revert to a survival mind-set and lose the strength that ought to be mine through You. I feel weak. I feel tired. I feel emotionally exhausted at the issues that rise up all around me.

Forgive me for giving in to my feelings more than turning to Your Word to find the strength that is mine in Your name. I want to know the manifestation of Your strength in my life on a greater level. Forgive me for failing to ask You for it as I should, especially in those moments I need it most.

Thanksgiving

Father, thank You for supplying strength to the weary. Thank You for showing Yourself strong by showing up in those who follow You.

You allow me to take action in the face of opposition. You give me the courage to speak up when I need to speak up. Thank You for blessing me with the abundance of Your strength when I ask for it. I want more of Your strength in my life. I want to witness what Your strength does both in and through me to make this world a better place for all of us. Thank You for giving me the opportunity to do that with my life.

Supplication

Lord, I ask for the wisdom I need to look to You for strength rather than relying on myself. I know I need to rest in Your strength and allow it to move through me. My strength becomes depleted at times. My strength runs out. But I want to live with the insight and wisdom that will enable me to rise up and live out my full destiny and purpose, God. I want to know what it is to live victoriously in times of desperation or in seasons of doubt. I want to overcome the obstacles the enemy hurls at me.

Show me how I can do this in a way that honors You and enables me to get to know You at a deeper level than ever before. I love and adore You.

In Jesus' name, I pray this prayer, asking to know You more through knowing Your ability to strengthen me. Amen.

41

Knowing God Through His Depths and Riches

*Oh, the depth of the riches both of the
wisdom and knowledge of God!
How unsearchable are His judgments and
unfathomable His ways!
FOR WHO HAS KNOWN THE MIND OF THE LORD,
OR WHO BECAME HIS COUNSELOR?
OR WHO HAS FIRST GIVEN TO HIM
THAT IT MIGHT BE PAID BACK TO HIM AGAIN?
For from Him and through Him
and to Him are all things.
To Him be the glory forever. Amen.*

ROMANS 11:33-36

Adoration

God Almighty, my prayer is to know the depth and riches of both Your wisdom and Your knowledge. That You allow and enable me to know both produces praise and worship in me. I lift up Your name in adoration as I glorify who You are. How unsearchable are Your judgments and how unfathomable are Your ways. Who has known Your mind, God? Who has become Your counselor? Who do You go to for advice? No one. Because You are over all, You see all, and You rule all.

To You be the glory forever and ever. For from You and through You and to You are all things. I worship Your abundant wisdom, depth, and riches, my God.

Confession

Holy Lord, today I confess to You that I don't always seek You as I should so I can explore and come to know You in a way You have made available to me. You are deep and unending, and yet at times I feel that I catch only a glimpse of You here or there. When times are tough and things become frightening, I go to You. But when life seems smooth, I often focus on my own wants and desires, dismissing knowing You as a continual journey where I am to pursue You at a deeper level.

Forgive me for neglecting my relationship with You time and time again. Let me feel the cleansing power of Your forgiveness as I confess the sin of spiritual apathy to You right now.

Thanksgiving

Father, thank You for making Yourself known in the greatest way to all who seek You. Thank You for allowing me the opportunity to know You fully and deeply for who You are. Please give me a greater awareness of who You are and a greater sensitivity toward knowing You. I want to explore the depths of Your thinking and discover those things that motivate and delight You. Show me how I can do that better each day.

Thank You that my prayers can reach You in powerful ways to produce powerful results. I pray that this prayer asking to know the depths of Your love be amplified in my spirit and answered by Yours.

Supplication

God, let me know the power of Your hope and the depth of Your love through a more authentic relationship with You. Show me how I can open my heart more in order to understand who You are more deeply. I adore You and love You, and I ask that You give me a more tender spirit so I can perceive those times when You are speaking to me. Cause me to fully realize Your love in a more personal and intimate way. Help me to look to You for my self-worth rather than to others. I ask that You will enable me to rest in Your love, especially in those times when I am feeling rejected or left out. I love You and pray this prayer in Jesus' name, amen.

42

Knowing God Through the Work of His Hands

The heavens are telling of the glory of God;
and their expanse is declaring the work of His hands.

PSALM 19:1

Adoration

Father, the heavens speak boldly of Your glory. I lift my hands in praise and worship You. Show me what Your creation reveals about You on a greater level than I have yet seen. I want to know the wonder of who You are, the glory of Your universe. Its expansiveness stretches beyond my own understanding. When I stare at the stars and look into the deep darkness around me in the night, my heart raises a hallelujah to Your name.

I worship You, the great God over all, whose glory is displayed across the sky.

Confession

God, make me know the bounty of Your grace on a greater and deeper level. I confess that the majesty of Your universe escapes me. I confess that I often fail to recognize the fullness of Your glory, and when I do, I focus more on myself than I ought. I walk before You in wonder, but

I confess that I don't always ascribe to You the confidence in Your glory that would produce rest in me.

Show me how to rest more fully in the grand glory of Your great power, which is revealed through the heavens. Forgive me for my anxious thoughts that cause me to concern myself with things that are beyond my scope of understanding. Your thoughts, Your ways, and Your glory are over all, and I need to reflect more fully on all three. Help me seek to do so every day.

Thanksgiving

Father, thank You for the greatness of who You are. Thank You for not hiding it tucked away and out of sight. Thank You for allowing me to live within Your creation, whose heavens speak loudly of Your glory.

I want to thank You today for the peace that comes to me when I consider Your glory and the scope of Your arm. You are magnificent in all ways. Receive the thanksgiving of my heart as I honor You with gratitude. The expanse of the universe and the vastness of the skies voice the beauty of Your great grace, might, and majesty. May glory be forever shouted from the heavens so loudly that I can't help but hear it and respond in praise and thanksgiving.

Supplication

God, I ask that You show me where to look in order to glimpse a more intimate view of Your glory. I ask that You cause me to understand on a deeper level who You truly are. Make me know Your heart and all that it contains so I can better reflect You in all I do.

Thank You, God, for the ability to pray to You and ask for Your leading in my knowing You. Open my eyes, Lord, that I may truly absorb and take in the vastness of Your Spirit and power.

In Christ's name, even as the heavens declare Your glory, I pray this prayer, acknowledging the vastness of who You are. Amen.

43

Knowing God Through Knowing His Son, Jesus Christ

No one has seen God at any time;
the only begotten God who is in the bosom of the Father,
He has explained Him.

JOHN 1:18

Adoration

Holy God, I look to You through the reflection of You in the Person of Jesus Christ. I lift up Your name in praise and worship because of the great love You have shown me through the revelation of Your Son. When I feel alone, You are near. When I think of giving up, You keep me going. This is because You are not some far-off and distant God with whom I have no contact. And because You have explained Yourself through the life of Christ, I worship You for giving me the ability to understand and know You through Him.

Confession

Father, I confess that I often create my own ideas of who You are rather than look to You in Christ to understand You fully. I put You in a box of my own understanding. Or sometimes I say You are too difficult to understand, and so I stop trying.

Instead, I should look to the revelation of the character of Christ. Forgive me for pulling back from You rather than running to You when I can't figure out things. Forgive me for forging ahead in my own understanding of who You are and what You desire rather than taking the time to explore Your heart and mind through the gift of the Spirit of Christ in me. Thank You for Your loving forgiveness and mercy.

Thanksgiving

God, thank You for the revelation and explanation of who You are through the Person of Jesus Christ. Thank You for sending Your Son into this world that we may come to know You more fully. Through Christ, we see into Your heart and Your mind more clearly than we could without Christ. Thank You for showing us a heart of love, compassion, peace, and power.

Thank You for enabling me to live according to Your will because I can be aware of Your will through Christ. As Christ explains You to me and to my spirit, I can reflect the image of God on a higher level than I could without knowing You deeply at all. Thank You for lifting me up higher because of Your great love that reveals Yourself to me through Jesus.

Supplication

God, explain Your heart to me on a deeper level. Allow me to understand and know You more fully. My eyes seek You today, Lord. I lift up my heart and my mind in an effort to pray to You so that I may know You more. Show me how to know You more through the Person of Jesus Christ. Help me recognize Your closeness and Your Spirit more regularly.

I ask that my awareness of You be expanded and that my knowledge of You be deepened according to the grace of Christ, who reveals Your mind, Your thoughts, and Your desires.

In the precious name of Jesus, I pray this prayer, praising You for the revelation of who You are through Your Son. Amen.

44

Knowing God Through His Demonstration of Love

God demonstrates His own love toward us,
in that while we were yet sinners,
Christ died for us.

ROMANS 5:8

Adoration

Holy God, the demonstration of Your love knows no bounds. While humanity was living in sin and apart from a loving relationship with You, You died for us. You demonstrate Your love in so many ways. You demonstrate Your love through Your provisions. You demonstrate Your love through Your grace. You demonstrate Your love through Your mercy. I worship You for the demonstration of Your love on so many levels.

I adore Your name, God. I lift up my praise to You as I see within You the depth of love no one else has ever shown me. The greatest love I've ever known has come from You, and I want to praise You with my heart and my mind and my whole life.

Confession

God, I ask for Your forgiveness because I know I don't honor the demonstration of Your love through the life of Jesus Christ the way I should. I don't pay enough attention to the depth of Your love, displayed through the sacrifice of Your Son.

Yet I barely take notice on most days. Instead, I complain about what others are doing or the difficult situations in my life. Forgive me for dismissing the greatest gift ever given to me and lacking a full awareness of Your character of love.

Thanksgiving

Father, thank You for the gift of Your love, demonstrated through the blood of the Lamb and given up for me on the cross. Thank You for taking notice of me and providing me with the way to eternal glory in Your name. I lift up Your heart of love in praise and thanksgiving. I know You will receive my thanksgiving with joy.

Supplication

God, I want to know the fullness of Your love because of the depth of Your love. Your love is so deep that You gave up Your Son on my behalf. I want to experience a love like this in every area of my life. When I'm scared, please calm my fears. When I'm lonely, be my comforter and guide. When I'm confused, provide clarity in my mind.

Let the fullness and overflowing of Your love fill my heart and overflow into my own life in how I relate to others. Will You give me a deeper love for those around me so I can reflect You and Your character in a better way? Will You show me ways I can demonstrate my love to others so they, too, can come to know You even more than they do now?

I thank You for hearing this prayer as, in Christ's name, I pray concerning the demonstration of Your love. Amen.

45

Knowing God Through His Word

All Scripture is inspired by God and profitable for teaching,
for reproof, for correction, for training in righteousness;
so that the man of God may be adequate,
equipped for every good work.

2 TIMOTHY 3:16-17

Adoration

Father, all Scripture is inspired by You, and You have given us Your Word for instruction. It's profitable for teaching, reproof, and correction—and to train me on how to live righteously. Your desire is for me to be equipped for every good work. I worship You for the way You have prepared me to learn through the truth found in the Bible. I worship You for giving me a hunger and a thirst for Your Word in order for me to learn what You have to say for myself.

I want to give You praise for giving us a tool that will also guide and direct us according to Your desires for our life. May Your name receive the glory and praise due You as evidenced through the worship of You recorded for us in the Word of God.

Confession

Father, You know my confession even before I speak it. You know I'm sorry that I don't spend as much time in Your Word as I ought. I could spend greater amounts of time there to develop myself more fully, both spiritually and emotionally.

Forgive me for the hours I waste on seemingly insignificant things when Your Word provides what I need to grow, mature, and gain wisdom and knowledge of You. You have given me the path to greater knowledge of You in the gift of Your Word. Forgive me for not seeking You there as much as I go to Scripture to seek answers for myself.

Thanksgiving

Holy God, thank You for the gift of the revelation of Your mind, Your heart, and Your Spirit through Your holy Word. Thank You for blessing me with the guidance and guidelines I need to live a victorious kingdom life. Thank You for providing me with the tool to greater awareness and understanding of who You are, what You desire, and what Your kingdom rule is over this earth.

I also want to thank You for those men and women of God whom You have raised up to teach Your Word through speaking, writing, and proclaiming. My heart is full of thanksgiving as I think on and meditate on Your precepts so graciously given, so that I may know You more and reflect You more authentically.

Supplication

God, I ask for a greater hunger for Your Word. Awaken in me both the desire to know You more and the desire to know Your Word more. But also awaken in me the will to act on those desires. Show me where to go in Your Word, the places that will reveal Your heart and Spirit to me. I want to know You more. Your Word is the pathway to doing that.

Walk me through the pages of Scripture so I can gain a greater understanding of the kingdom agenda You seek for us to live out in every way. I want to honor You with my life choices, so I pray that You will shed light and wisdom into my spirit to show me the way to do that.

God, I praise You and thank You for the access I have to You through prayer, just as I do as I pray this prayer today. In Jesus' name, amen.

46

Knowing God Through His Fullness

Thus says the LORD, the King of Israel
and his Redeemer, the LORD of hosts:
"I am the first and I am the last,
and there is no God besides Me."

ISAIAH 44:6

Adoration

Holy God, You are the King of Israel, and You are my Redeemer. I worship the Lord of hosts who sits above all. You look down from the heavens to see Your creation. It is vast. It is populated. It is thriving with life. You made this. You created this. You spoke this into existence. Your love provides all we need to live.

Your love is also the hope in our hearts. Without You, all is darkness and lost. Your fullness exists everywhere. You are the first, and You are the last. There is no God besides You. You, my God, are the one and only God. Many gods seek to compete with You, but none can stand against You in any form. In the end, each one falls. You cut off the head of the enemy with one swoop because You are the great God with whom no one competes successfully at all.

Confession

God, I confess that, at times, I look to idols and dismiss Your rightful place in my heart as the first and the last. And I confess that I forget Your power when it appears that the enemy has risen stronger against You than You can defend. Or I cower in fear when the enemy comes toward me, forgetting I'm safe, secure, and victorious in Your armor provided to me through Your precious love.

Forgive me for forgetting that my own strength is rooted and grounded in Your fullness and that I have no lack. Forgive me for worry, anxiety, and hopelessness when I allow my life to be consumed by the enemy's schemes. You are the great and mighty King, and You are my Redeemer. I am to take comfort and find courage in this truth.

Thanksgiving

Thank You, God, for the fullness of who You are. Thank You for never lacking wisdom, power, or strength. You are above all and see all, which allows me to rest in the stability of Your overwhelming control. When things seem out of control to me, that's only because I don't have all the information.

Nothing is ever out of Your control. You are working behind the scenes to advance Your kingdom agenda on earth. Sometimes things need to be shaken up before they can be settled, and I want to thank You for Your loving hand that moves things in life to where they need to be. I may not always understand the process, but I trust Your heart.

Supplication

Lord, I lift up Your name in honor and respect as I ask You to help me know Your fullness even more than I do now. I want to know what it means to trust in Your strength and finality. You are the first, and You are the last. You know the beginning from the end. Nothing catches You by surprise, for You are the great God who sits over all.

Let me gain greater glimpses into Your work and Your ways so I can come to know You and find the peace You give in times of uncertainty. When I remember You are working out things for good, I can rest in the midst of difficulties and trying times. Help me know—more deeply in my spirit—the assurance of Your fullness as God.

I love You, Lord, and according to the power of Jesus Christ, I pray to know You more through Your fullness. Amen.

Knowing God Through His Plurality

God said, "Let Us make man in Our image,
according to Our likeness;
and let them rule over the fish of the sea and
over the birds of the sky and over the cattle and
over all the earth, and over every creeping
thing that creeps on the earth."

GENESIS 1:26

Adoration

Holy God, I praise You and worship You, for Your triune being comprises the Father, the Son, and the Spirit. You are one God, but You are made up of three coequal parts. No part of You is more valuable than any other, and each part carries out a distinct role in pursuing the advancement of Your kingdom agenda on earth.

I worship You for the complex nature of who You are. I lift up Your name in praise for the diversity represented in Your very self. You carry all the attributes that make for a peaceful, righteous, and hope-filled world. I love how You love us enough to give us insight into Your nature and personhood, using Yourself as a model for how we should all get along and unify in the body of Christ. Let my voice be a constant unifier in all I say and do.

Confession

God, while I understand Your plurality in many ways, I don't always access or maximize my relationship with You across the triune personhood of Your being. This is my fault for looking only at what appeals to me or is comfortable to me while ignoring areas that bring me discomfort or confusion.

Forgive me for picking and choosing which parts of You I want to know and relate to rather than seeking to relate to You in Your pluralistic, triune nature of God the Father, Christ the Son, and the Holy Spirit. I want to know You more, and that includes knowing those parts of You with which I haven't spent time meditating on or abiding in.

Thanksgiving

Lord God, thank You for the beauty of Your plurality securely brought together in the individual nature of Your being as the one true God. You are made up of three coequal parts, and yet You are one God. The unity within You is so deeply connected that You have given me insight into how I am to be with other believers.

Thank You for loving me from all aspects of Your being. Thank You for leading me and guiding me as well as protecting me and teaching me. Thank You for correcting me and encouraging me. Your triune self allows me to experience many aspects of Your nature as I relate to all parts of You.

Supplication

God, I ask that You lead me and guide me on how I can better know each aspect of You and all of Your character qualities on a deeper level. Show me how to relate to You as God the Father. Let me increase my time abiding with Jesus Christ the Son. Open my heart to Your Holy Spirit so I come to recognize His voice speaking to me and leading me.

I come boldly to You right now and ask for a supernatural gift of Your grace, which will enable me to know You more holistically. You alone are the one true God comprising three coequal persons who demonstrate love, mercy, and peace as You relate to Your creation.

God, I want to know You more as, according to the name of Jesus Christ, I pray this prayer recognizing Your triune being. Amen.

48

Knowing God Through His Distinctions

*The grace of the Lord Jesus Christ, and the love of God,
and the fellowship of the Holy Spirit,
be with you all.*

2 CORINTHIANS 13:14

Adoration

God, Your plurality allows great distinctions in who You are. You are the fullness of the Father. You are the completeness of Christ. And You are the wholeness of the Holy Spirit. Each part reflects an aspect of You that gives me all I need for my life.

I praise Your name and the reflection of Your character in each of Your distinct persons of the holy Trinity. My worship extends to the heavens, where I bless the name of the Father, the name of the Son, and the name of the Spirit. Receive the honor that comes from my heart as I humbly bow before You, knowing You more and more each day through the revelation of Your attributes, known through Your triune nature.

Confession

Father, Jesus, and Spirit, I confess my one-directional awareness of You as I pray. Oftentimes, I direct my thoughts and my prayers to God the Father while dismissing the valuable interaction and relationship afforded me through Jesus and through the Spirit.

Please forgive me for keeping my focus limited to what I know and understand rather than seeking to expand my understanding and knowing You more holistically. Forgive me for being quick about my prayers as well, rather than taking my time to explore Your heart and Your will as manifested through the distinct persons of the Trinity.

Thanksgiving

Thank You, Lord, for allowing me to pray to You in such a way that will help me get to know You better and more completely. Thank You for placing in me a desire to know You more. I want to know each part of You as well as I know the others. The mercy of Christ and the compassion of the Spirit are to be my guides as I come to You boldly, before Your throne of great grace.

Thank You that I can come to You in this way and seek to connect to You in a more meaningful way than I ever have before.

Supplication

God, show me broader glimpses into Your heart about who You are and how You reveal Your distinct traits through the triune nature of the Father, Son, and the Spirit. Help me to come to know what You desire me to know about You so my prayers can be more effective.

May the Holy Spirit convict me of sins I don't even know I need to confess so I can be made right with You. I want others to know You more fully, too, so I pray You will develop in me a greater confidence in being a mouthpiece for Your truth and a sharer of Your love to those with whom I come into contact.

I pray all of these things in the name of the Father, the Son, and the Holy Spirit. Amen.

49

Knowing God Through His Oneness

*That they may all be one; even as You, Father,
are in Me and I in You, that they also may be in Us,
so that the world may believe that You sent Me.*

John 17:21

Adoration

Father, unity is who You are. You distinctly comprise a triune of beings, but unity makes up Your mission and core. You are one with Christ. You are one with the Spirit. As well, You desire for me to be one with You and one with others through the bond of Christ.

I praise You, for You are the perfect model of what our world so desperately needs. Because of all of the division between people today, which keeps our unity at a distance, I ask You to show Yourself strong to truly unify us as one in You and one with one another in love.

Confession

God, I understand that You value unity, and I'm grateful for Your kingdom rule that establishes unity and oneness, not only with You but also with others. But I don't always live up to the prayer Jesus prayed in John 17. I confess that I lack the pure love that always turns the other cheek.

I confess that I have not initiated efforts toward creating greater unity in the body of Christ.

Forgive me for the times my words divided rather than united. Forgive me for the things I've said that didn't reflect the unified oneness You are as God and that You want to display through us, Your church. I ask for Your great grace, as I know oneness is an important facet of advancing Your kingdom agenda on earth.

Thanksgiving

Lord God, thank You that I can be one with You, as is Christ. Thank You that You even desire that level of closeness with me. I know that as I come to know You more and grow closer to You in a unified way, the oneness I experience with You will bring me greater levels of peace, assurance, and clarity.

Thank You for the calm that comes in uniting with You in spirit. Thank You for the freedom from fear You provide as I draw closer to You in an authentic relationship with You rooted in mutual love. Thank You that I can be used by You to model oneness to a world fractured by hate, pride, and ego. I ask that You make me a balm of unity to those who need to experience it most, and I thank You for using me in this way.

Supplication

Father, as I come to You more fully and experience You more deeply, I ask that You develop a greater love in my heart for others. Let me shine Your love to others in such a way that they will overflow with a desire to become one with You as well. Give me a greater level of empathy and compassion for others as they walk the journey to knowing You. Help me not to judge. Rather, enable me to extend kindness in ways that reveal Your heart to them.

There is so much pain in the world, God. People need You. People need to be one with You. Will You make me a wayshower for how they can come to know You more fully and experience Your presence more deeply?

In Jesus' name and because He prayed, I ask for oneness with You and oneness with others. And I ask that others may be one with You as well. Amen.

50

Knowing God Through His Revelations

When He, the Spirit of truth, comes,
He will guide you into all the truth;
for He will not speak on His own initiative,
but whatever He hears, He will speak;
and He will disclose to you what is to come.

JOHN 16:13

Adoration

Heavenly Father, I praise You for Your revelatory nature. You make known all things I need to know through the love of the Holy Spirit. And as the Spirit of truth lives in me, I know I can access truth whenever I want to. I worship You for this gift within me that enables me to combat the schemes of the enemy. Your Holy Spirit guides me into all truth. Your Spirit does not speak on His own initiative but rather speaks what He hears from You in order to disclose it to me. In fact, Your Word says that the Spirit will even disclose things that are to come.

I adore You and honor Your name, for You are truly past, present, and future into one moment of right now. You know all things. You know what is to come. And to those who have an ear to hear and a heart to understand, You declare all things from the end to the beginning.

Confession

Lord, please forgive me for worrying about tomorrow. Forgive me for failing to abide with the Holy Spirit on a deeper level so I can receive all I need by way of truth. I sometimes become confused or feel anxious when I hear about all that is going on in the world today. Yet I need to take more time placing what I hear against the backdrop of truth given through Your disclosure to me from the Holy Spirit.

Give me abundant grace and mercy as I seek Your Spirit's guidance in my life more than I have ever done before. Give me the grace to know You more fully. And give me the mercy I need for having dismissed You and Your truth and disclosure for so long.

Thanksgiving

Thank You, God, for truth comes from You. Truth rolls down to us from high, enlightening our hearts and minds with all we need to know and understand. Thank You for not hiding truth nor disclosures of what is to come. Rather, You have established a way for each of us to know more through the gift of Your Holy Spirit.

Will You show me how to grow in my awareness of the truth I need to know in order to make wise choices? I thank You in advance for the way You teach me through the power of Your Spirit and His presence in my life.

Supplication

Father, open my eyes that I may see You more clearly and recognize the truth among the lies that pop up in our world. Give me discernment so I can take all thoughts captive to the character of Jesus Christ. Let my heart be an instrument of abiding with Your Spirit at such depth that I quickly recognize truth from fiction. Please surround me with individuals who will speak Your truth into my life when they notice I'm off track from the way of Your Word.

I also ask that I'll be a voice to speak truth and life into the darkness of these evil days that have come upon us on earth. Let me use the opportunities You give me to help others to want to draw closer to You—and closer to the Spirit, who gives truth and revelation to each of us.

I pray this prayer in the truth-bearing name of Jesus Christ. Amen.

51

Knowing God Through His Pleasure

Behold, a voice out of the heavens said,
"This is My beloved Son,
in whom I am well-pleased."

MATTHEW 3:17

Adoration

Lord, I come to You today in humility as I seek to honor You through my prayer. I worship You today with a full heart, knowing You are not some robotic form sitting elsewhere looking on. You are a God of emotion. You take pleasure and delight in things, and You experience a range of emotions.

When the Spirit's dove descended upon Jesus in the Jordan, You spoke of being well-pleased with Him. You spoke of endearment. You spoke of satisfaction. You spoke with the voice of command and grace mixed into one. And in doing so, You sought to make us know how You felt about Him. You revealed to us a side of Yourself that Scripture doesn't always frequently show.

I praise and worship You for giving me the ability to enter into Your pleasure and to cause You to smile through what I do and say.

Confession

Lord, forgive me for boxing You in at times. In those situations where I neglect to relate to You as a loving God, instead perceiving You as some distant being who has no real emotive connection to me, I lean toward others for advice or comfort. Yet You are the God of all comfort, and You take delight in a great many things.

Forgive me for not celebrating with You in times of celebration. Forgive me for forgetting to consider the reality that I can cause You to smile. Forgive me, Lord, for choosing things that bring pleasure only to me over and above what will also bring You pleasure.

Thanksgiving

God, thank You for Your forgiveness. Thank You for Your love. Thank You for being a God who takes delight and pleasure. Like a parent, You experience satisfaction when my choices align with Your will. And may Your heart be full of satisfaction and pleasure as You look upon Your body of believers.

I give You the thanksgiving of my heart, knowing I can relate to You in so many ways. I can speak to You as I speak to a friend. I can laugh with You as well. Lord, help me know Your emotive side more so I can draw nearer to You in joy.

Supplication

Heavenly Father, I want to know Your pleasure. I want to hear You say of me that You are "well pleased." I want to experience the satisfaction of Your satisfaction over me.

Help me see You for who You truly are. Enlighten my heart and my mind to understand Your emotions more and to take down the guard I sometimes put up between us. Let me come boldly to You in raw feeling and honesty, because that's what You desire from me. I also want to make You satisfied with the choices I make and the words I speak. Set a seal on my heart so my heart's love goes only to You in worship. In that way, as I draw closer to You in everything I do, feel, think, and say, I enter into a deeper relationship with You.

I love You, Lord, and I pray to You in the name of the Son in whom You are well pleased. Amen.

52

Knowing God Through His Honor

The LORD God of Israel declares,
"I did indeed say that
your house and the house of your father
should walk before Me forever";
but now the LORD declares, "Far be it from Me—
for those who honor Me
I will honor, and those who despise
Me will be lightly esteemed."

1 SAMUEL 2:30

Adoration

God, I come to You in prayer with a heart full of honor for who You are. I honor You for the many ways You have made Yourself known to me during the trials and tests of my life. I honor You for Your loving care when I needed it the most. I honor You, for You are holy and deserving of all honor. You sit high above all else, on the throne, and rule as the King over all. You are deserving of all of my honor and worship.

Receive this praise I give You today because I desire for it to please You. I want to please You in how I pray to You, in what I think, in what I say, and in what I do. When I please You, I'm honoring You through my being. Let me represent and reflect You in such a manner that brings You honor and points other people to You.

Confession

God, I haven't always honored You from the heart. Sometimes I say the words, but the honor is far from them. Other times my actions demonstrate that I'm not concerned about honoring You in what I do. You are all-powerful. You are mighty. You are honorable. Yet I don't always hold You in the high esteem that is rightfully Yours.

Forgive me for the dismissive nature of my flesh. Forgive me for the focus I place on myself and on honoring my own achievements rather than giving You the glory You should have from me.

Thanksgiving

Thank You, God, for revealing Your nature to me in such a way that causes me to come to know You more fully. As I do, as I come to know You more closely, honor wells up inside of me. I desire to honor You in both word and deed.

Thank You for seeding this desire in me and for cultivating it so that it has grown over time. Thank You for being honorable, caring, loving, and true. Thank You for setting the standard for what it means to make choices reflecting a character of dignity and grace. Thank You for modeling for me all I need in order to know how to live a life of honor.

God, receive my thanks from an authentic space of pure honor for who You truly are.

Supplication

Father, I ask to know Your honor even more than I do right now. Show me Your ways. Reveal to me Your acts. Give me insight into Your strategies for bringing good and light into a darkened world. Help me gain greater glimpses into Your heart of honor so I can be lifted up to live a life that is more honorable as well. I want to be as close a reflection of You as I can be, so I pray You will season my words with grace and compassion at all times.

Father, help me forgive myself for those times and seasons I didn't honor You as I knew I should. Help me to live in boldness, knowing that Your forgiveness has made all things new and that I can rightly live according to Your precepts and kingdom principles.

In the matchless name of Jesus Christ, I pray this prayer, all in honor of You. Amen.

53

Knowing God Through His Satisfying Power

The LORD will continually guide you,
and satisfy your desire in scorched places,
and give strength to your bones;
and you will be like a watered garden,
and like a spring of water whose waters do not fail.

ISAIAH 58:11

Adoration

Father God, You alone can bring satisfaction to my needs when I'm in want. You are my Shepherd who causes me to lie down in green pastures. You lead me through the valley and guide me to a safe space where I can reflect and rest.

I praise You because You know how to satisfy my desire when I'm in scorched places. I worship You because You provide strength to my bones and my spirit in such a way that causes me to rise up like a watered garden and bear fruit in all I do. Your love never fails. It's a spring of water continually pouring out the grace, peace, wisdom, and satisfaction I need to face each day with a spirit of enjoyment and delight. Despite the trials and troubles that surround me, my eyes and my heart are filled with hope because of You and Your presence in my life.

Confession

Lord, I confess my lack of gratitude for all You give me and provide me. I confess and ask for Your forgiveness for the many gifts from You I simply take for granted. Help me not be so busy that I fail to notice the ways You lift my spirit and infuse my soul with love, especially in those times when hope wanes.

Please forgive me for focusing so much of my attention on the things in life that don't produce true satisfaction and peace.

Thanksgiving

Thank You, Holy God, for the way You provide life and love to me, satisfying my soul with the finest of Your peace. Thank You for being just a prayer away. When I reach out my hand for Your help, Your hand is already in mine, offering the gifts of grace and the peace of perspective.

Thank You for the joy that comes from above, which gives me strength. You are the strength of my soul and my portion forever. Thank You for always being present, for always being willing to engage, and for always allowing me the opportunity to call out to You when I'm out of strength.

Supplication

Lord, give me great satisfaction in my work. Give me delight in the career in which I spend so much time. I ask You to help me find the delight that's present in carrying out the tasks at hand. I don't want to waste time just working for a paycheck. Rather, help me find the joy You supply in every aspect of life.

Fill me with delight and strengthen my soul. Let me be a light of love to those around me. Let me honor and worship You through being a brighter reflection of who You are to those in need.

In Christ's name, I pray this prayer as I seek to know You more by fully recognizing the delight and satisfaction You supply. Amen.

54

Knowing God Through His Overarching Power

The LORD is the true God;
He is the living God and the everlasting King.
At His wrath the earth quakes,
and the nations cannot endure His indignation.
Thus you shall say to them,
"The gods that did not make the heavens
and the earth will perish from the earth
and from under the heavens."
It is He who made the earth by His power,
who established the world
by His wisdom; and by His understanding
He has stretched out the heavens.
When He utters His voice,
there is a tumult of waters in the heavens,
and He causes the clouds to ascend from the end of the earth;
He makes lightning for the rain, and brings
out the wind from His storehouses.

JEREMIAH 10:10-13

Adoration

Holy God, as I come to know You more fully, I stand amazed at Your overarching power. I stand in awe at how great You truly are.

You are the living God and the everlasting King. Your wrath causes the earth to tremble. No nation can endure Your indignation. You rule over all, and no enemy has the power to overtake You. I praise You because You are the One who made the earth by Your overarching power. You established the world through Your wisdom. You stretched out the heavens through Your awareness and understanding of how things truly work and hold together. When You speak, tumult takes place within the waters in the heavens, causing the clouds to come to earth. You form the lightning. You bring the rain and the wind. You are over all.

Confession

God, I want to know more of Your overarching power. Forgive me for any lack within me that sidesteps my pursuit of You with full passion. Forgive me for any dismissive attitude I have toward You. Forgive me for failing to give You the honor, praise, and awe that are rightfully Yours. You alone are God Almighty. You alone are King over all.

Please show me Your greater grace in growing me to a fuller awareness of Your overarching power and in forgiving my judgments, self-focus, and pride.

Thanksgiving

Thank You, God, for Your strength that supplies all I need to carry out the calling You have placed on my life. Thank You for giving me a purpose You can use to bring greater glory to You. Thank You that Your power in me enables me to advance Your kingdom agenda on earth.

I also want to thank You for raising up a generation of believers who are also seeking Your kingdom and Your will—and who want to be a light of Your love to a world of darkness. Receive my thanks as it comes couched in a spirit of humility, knowing that Your overarching power enables me to be here right now and pray to You right now.

I love You, Lord, and I thank You with all my heart.

Supplication

Father, quicken in me a stronger desire to know Your overarching power in my life. Enlighten my eyes with the ability to see Your spiritual work in my heart and in the circumstances I find myself in. Will You help me become a mouthpiece that speaks Your truth to the world at large? Give me wisdom and insight into how to do that more effectively.

I also ask You to awaken a greater number of people in the body of Christ so they will desire to know You more than they ever have before. Raise up spiritual leaders who will guide us into Your heart of wisdom and power, so that, collectively, we can have a more effective impact on our society.

God, I pray this prayer asking to more fully know You through Your overarching power. In Jesus' name, amen.

The Urban Alternative

The Urban Alternative (TUA) equips, empowers, and unites Christians to impact *individuals, families, churches,* and *communities* through a thoroughly kingdom agenda worldview. In teaching truth, we seek to transform lives.

The core cause of the problems we face in our personal lives, homes, churches, and societies is a spiritual one; therefore, the only way to address it is spiritually. We've tried a political, social, economic, and even a religious agenda.

It's time for a kingdom agenda.

The kingdom agenda can be defined as the visible manifestation of the comprehensive rule of God over every area of life.

The unifying central theme throughout the Bible is the glory of God and the advancement of His kingdom. The conjoining thread from Genesis to Revelation—from beginning to end—is focused on one thing: God's glory through advancing God's kingdom.

When you do not recognize that theme, the Bible becomes disconnected stories that are great for inspiration but seem to be unrelated in purpose and direction. Understanding the role of the kingdom in Scripture increases the relevancy of this several-thousand-year-old text to your day-to-day living because the kingdom is not only then, it is now.

The absence of the kingdom's influence in our personal and family lives, churches and communities has led to a deterioration in our world of immense proportions:

- People live segmented, compartmentalized lives because they lack God's kingdom worldview.
- Families disintegrate because they exist for their own satisfaction rather than for the kingdom.
- Churches are limited in the scope of their impact because they fail to comprehend that the goal of the church is not the church itself but the kingdom.
- Communities have nowhere to turn to find real solutions for real people who have real problems because the church has become divided, in-grown, and unable to transform the cultural landscape in any relevant way.

The kingdom agenda offers us a way to see and live life with a solid hope by optimizing the solutions of heaven. When God is no longer the final and authoritative standard under which all else falls, order and hope leave with Him. But the reverse of that is true as well: as long as you have God, you have hope. If God is still in the picture, and as long as His agenda is still on the table, it's not over.

Even if relationships collapse, God will sustain you. Even if finances dwindle, God will keep you. Even if dreams die, God will revive you. As long as God and His rule are still the overarching rule in your life, family, church, and community, there is always hope.

Our world needs the King's agenda. Our churches need the King's agenda. Our families need the King's agenda.

We've put together a three-part plan to direct us to heal the divisions and strive for unity as we move toward the goal of truly being one nation under God. This three-part plan calls us to assemble with others in unity, address the issues that divide us, and to act together for social impact. Following this plan, we will see individuals, families, churches, and communities transformed as we follow God's kingdom agenda in every area of our lives.

In many major cities, there is a loop that drivers can take when they want to get somewhere on the other side of the city but don't necessarily want to head straight through downtown. This loop will take you close enough to the city so you can see its towering buildings and skyline but not close enough to actually experience it.

This is precisely what we, as a culture, have done with God. We have put Him on the "loop" of our personal, family, church, and community lives. He's close enough to be at hand should we need Him in an emergency, but He's far enough away that He can't be the center of who we are.

We want God on the "loop," not the King of the Bible who comes downtown into the very heart of our ways. Leaving God on the "loop" brings about dire consequences, as we have seen in our own lives and with others. But when we make God, and His rule, the centerpiece of all we think, do, or say, then we will experience Him in the way He longs to be experienced by us.

He wants us to be kingdom people with kingdom minds set on fulfilling His kingdom's purposes. He wants us to pray, as Jesus did, "Not my will, but Thy will be done." Because His is the kingdom, the power, and the glory.

There is only one God, and we are not Him. As King and Creator, God calls the shots. It is only when we align ourselves beneath His comprehensive hand that we will access His full power and authority in all spheres of life: personal, familial, ecclesiastical, and societal.

As we learn how to govern ourselves under God, we then transform the institutions of family, church, and society from a biblically based kingdom worldview.

Under Him, we touch heaven and change earth.

To achieve our goal, we use a variety of strategies, approaches, and resources for reaching and equipping as many people as possible.

Broadcast Media

Millions of individuals experience *The Alternative with Dr. Tony Evans* through the daily radio broadcast playing on nearly 1,400 RADIO outlets and in more than 130 countries. The broadcast can also be seen on several television networks, and it is viewable online at TonyEvans .org. You can also listen to or view the daily broadcast by downloading the Tony Evans app for free in the App store. More than 20,000,000 message downloads/streams occur each year.

Leadership Training

The Tony Evans Training Center (TETC) facilitates educational programming that embodies the ministry philosophy of Dr. Tony Evans as expressed through the kingdom agenda. The training courses focus on leadership development and discipleship in the following five tracks:

- Bible and theology
- personal growth
- family and relationships
- church health and leadership development
- society and community impact strategies

The TETC program includes courses for both local and online students. Furthermore, TETC programming includes course work for nonstudent attendees. Pastors, Christian leaders, and Christian laity, both local and at a distance, can seek out the Kingdom Agenda Certificate for personal, spiritual, and professional development. For more information, visit: tonyevanstraining.org.

The Kingdom Agenda Pastors (KAP) provides a *viable network* for *like-minded pastors* who embrace the kingdom agenda philosophy. Pastors have the opportunity to go deeper with Dr. Tony Evans as they are given greater biblical knowledge, practical applications, and resources to impact individuals, families, churches, and communities. KAP welcomes *senior and associate pastors* of all churches. KAP also offers an annual summit held each year in Dallas with intensive seminars, workshops, and resources.

Pastors' Wives Ministry, founded by Dr. Lois Evans, provides *counsel, encouragement*, and *spiritual resources* for pastors' wives as they serve with their husbands in the ministry. A primary focus of the ministry is the KAP Summit that offers senior pastors' wives a safe place to *reflect, renew*, and *relax* along with training in personal development, spiritual growth, and care for their emotional and physical well-being.

Community and Cultural Influence

National Church Adopt-A-School Initiative (NCAASI) prepares churches across the country to impact communities by using *public schools as the primary vehicle for effecting positive social change* in urban youth and families. Leaders of churches, school districts, faith-based organizations, and other nonprofit organizations are equipped with the knowledge and tools to *forge partnerships* and build *strong social service delivery systems*. This training is based on the comprehensive church-based community impact strategy conducted by Oak Cliff Bible Fellowship. It addresses such areas as economic development, education, housing, health revitalization, family renewal, and racial reconciliation. We assist churches in tailoring the model to meet the specific needs of their communities while simultaneously addressing the spiritual and moral frame of reference. Training events are held annually in the Dallas area at Oak Cliff Bible Fellowship.

Athlete's Impact (AI) exists as an outreach both into and through the sports arena. Coaches are the most influential factor in young people's lives, even ahead of their parents. With the growing rise of fatherlessness in our culture, more young people are looking to their coaches for guidance, character development, practical needs, and hope. After coaches on the influencer scale fall athletes. Athletes (whether professional or amateur) influence younger athletes and kids within their spheres of impact. Knowing this, we have made it our aim to equip and train coaches and athletes on how to live out and utilize their God-given roles for the benefit of the kingdom. We aim to do this through our iCoach App as well as through resources such as *The Playbook: A Life Strategy Guide for Athletes.*

Tony Evans Films ushers in positive life change through compelling video-shorts, animation, and feature-length films. We seek to build kingdom disciples through the power of story. We use a variety of platforms for viewer consumption and have more than 50,000,000 digital views. We also merge video-shorts and film with relevant Bible study materials to bring people to the saving knowledge of Jesus Christ and to strengthen the body of Christ worldwide. *Tony Evans Films* released the first feature-length film, *Kingdom Men Rising*, in April 2019, in more than 800 theaters nationwide, in partnership with Lifeway Films. The second release, *Journey with Jesus*, is in partnership with Right Now Media and filmed in Israel.

Resource Development

We are fostering lifelong learning partnerships with the people we serve by providing a variety of published materials. Dr. Evans has published more than 100 unique titles based on over 50 years of preaching, whether that is in booklet, book, or Bible study format. He also holds the honor of writing and publishing the first full-Bible commentary and Study Bible by an African American, released in 2019. This Bible sits in permanent display as a historic release in the Museum of the Bible in Washington, DC.

For more information and a complimentary copy of Dr. Evans'
devotional newsletter,
call (800) 800-3222 *or* write TUA at P.O. Box 4000, Dallas, TX
75208, *or* visit us online at
www.TonyEvans.org

The Doctrine of God

(Note: First appeared in the Oak Cliff Bible Fellowship Leadership Manual, 2001)

I. The Knowledge of God

A. The Concept of Knowing God

1. It involves the acquisition of accurate facts about God. (John 17:17; 2 Timothy 3:16-17)
2. It involves a saving encounter with God. (John 3:3; 1 John 5:20)
3. It involves an ongoing intimacy with God. (2 Peter 1:5-8; 3:18)
4. It involves personal experiences with God. (James 1:2-5; 1 Peter 1:6-7; 5:10)

B. The Possibility of Knowing God

1. God commands us to know Him. (Jeremiah 9:23-24)
2. God desires to be known intimately. (Exodus 33:11; Psalm 25:14)
3. God has prescribed a way to know Him. (Acts 2:40-47)
   - worship
   - fellowship
   - education
   - outreach
4. God has limitations on what can be known about Him. (Isaiah 40:12-14; 45:15; Deuteronomy 29:29)

5. God has given believers the Holy Spirit to reveal the things of God. (John 16:13-15; 1 Corinthians 2:10)

C. The Importance of Knowing God

1. It is the only way a person can escape judgment and enter into eternal life. (John 17:3)

2. It is the only way a person can truly know themselves. (Isaiah 6:5)

3. It is the best way of having an accurate knowledge of the world. (Romans 1:20; Colossians 1:15-17)

4. It is essential for personal holiness. (Jeremiah 9:23-24)

5. It enables people to be strong as they face the challenges of life. (Daniel 11:32)

6. It generates the true worship of God. (Romans 11:33-36)

II. The Revelation of God

A. Naturalistic Arguments for God's Existence

1. Argument of Cause-Effect (Cosmological)
   - For every effect there must be a cause, thus there must be a powerful cause for the existence of the universe. This argument does not prove that the cause is the Christian's God, but it does prove that the cause is powerful.

2. Argument of Purpose (Teleological)
   - There is definite order and design in the universe (seasons, Earth rotating on axis, planets revolving around the sun, etc.). Thus, the first cause must be intelligent. Just as a watch proves there must exist a watchmaker.

3. Argument from the Nature of Man (Anthropological)
   - Man's conscience, moral nature (sense of right and wrong), intelligence, and mental capacities have to be accounted for. His creator must thus bear these same qualities of personhood. Personal existence must have a personal source.

4. Argument from the Idea of God (Ontological)
   - Man has the idea of a most perfect being (where did that idea come from given the imperfections of man and the universe?), and since a most perfect being who does not exist is not as perfect as one that does exist, there must be a God.

B. Biblical Arguments for God's Existence
   1. General Revelation (that which is universally available in creation to all mankind)
      - Creation reveals God's glory and power. (Psalm 19:1)
      - Creation reveals God's supremacy and divine nature. (Romans 1:20)
      - Creation reveals God's providential control of nature. (Acts 14:17)
      - Creation reveals God's goodness. (Matthew 5:45)
      - Creation reveals God's intelligence. (Acts 17:24-29)
      - Creation reveals God's existence. (Acts 17:24-28)
      - Man's conscience universally affirms the existence of God. (Romans 1:19)

   2. Special Revelation (that which is limited to Jesus Christ and the Bible)
      - Jesus Christ is the supreme and final revelation of God to man. (Hebrews 1:1-2)
      - Jesus Christ "exegetes" (explains) the Person of God. (John 1:18)
      - Jesus Christ reveals the glory of God. (John 1:14)
      - Jesus Christ reveals the power and wisdom of God. (1 Corinthians 1:24)
      - Jesus Christ reveals the grace of God. (Titus 2:11)
      - Jesus Christ reveals the love of God. (Romans 5:8)
      - The Bible assumes and does not seek to prove the existence of God. (Genesis 1:1; Psalm 14:1; Hebrews 11:6)

- The Bible is the inerrant revelation of God. (2 Timothy 3:16-17)

III. The Triunity of God

A. The Definition of the Trinity—*Trinity* is a theological term (not a biblical one) used to describe the biblical teaching of the nature of God. It means there is one God composed of three coequal Persons who are one in essence yet distinct in personality. Thus God is three-in-one (like a pretzel).

B. The Delineation of Trinity
  1. There is only one true God. (Deuteronomy 6:4; Isaiah 44:6; John 17:3; 1 Corinthians 8:4)
  2. There is plurality in God. (Isaiah 48:16; 63:7-10; Genesis 1:26-27)
     - The Father is recognized as God. (John 6:27; 1 Peter 1:2)
     - Jesus Christ is recognized as God. (Titus 2:13; Hebrews 1:8; John 1:1,14,18)
     - The Holy Spirit is recognized as God. (1 Corinthians 3:16; Acts 5:3-4)
  3. These three are distinct persons.
     - The Father and the Son are distinct persons. (John 5:20,32,37; 17:5)
     - The Father and the Son are distinct from the Spirit. (John 14:16; 15:26)
  4. These three are unified. (Matthew 28:19; 3:12-16; 2 Corinthians 13:14)

C. The Work of the Trinity
  1. The Trinity works together to provide salvation. (Ephesians 1:7-9; 1 Corinthians 6:19-21; John 6:63)
  2. The Trinity works together in the revelation of God's truth. (John 1:17-18; 16:13)

3. The Trinity works together in prayer. (John 14:14; Ephesians 1:6; 2:18; 6:18)

4. The Trinity works together in creation. (Genesis 1:1-3,26; Colossians 1:16)

5. The Trinity works together in confirmation. (Matthew 3:16-17)

D. The Praise of the Trinity

1. The Father glorifies the Son. (John 6:37-40; Ephesians 1:4)

2. The Son honors the Father. (John 5:19,30-31; 12:28)

3. The Spirit honors the Son. (John 15:26; 16:8-10,14)

E. The Essence of the Trinity—All three members of the Trinity possess the attributes or perfection of deity.

IV. The Character of God

A. The Infinity of God—The infinity of God means He is eternal with no limitations except those imposed by His own nature, nor is He bound by the succession of events. (Psalm 90:2)

B. The Self-existence of God—The self-existence of God means that He does not depend on anyone or anything outside Himself for His life. (Jeremiah 10:10-13)

C. The Transcendence of God—The transcendence of God means that He is totally distinct and independent from His creation. (Isaiah 55:8-9)

D. The Sufficiency of God—The sufficiency of God means that He is totally and absolutely complete within Himself. (Acts 7:24-25)

E. The Holiness of God—The holiness of God means that His intrinsic and transcendent purity is the standard of righteousness to which the whole universe must conform. (1 Peter 1:13-19)

F. The Sovereignty of God—The sovereignty of God refers to His rule and control over all of His creation. (Daniel 4:28-37)

G. The Glory of God—The glory of God is the visible manifestation of His attributes. (Exodus 33:12-23)

H. The Omniscience of God—The omniscience of God refers to His intuitive knowledge of all things both actual and potential. (Psalm 139:1-6)

I. The Omnipresence of God—The omnipresence of God means that His complete essence is fully present in all places at all times. (Psalm 139:7-12)

J. The Omnipotence of God—The omnipotence of God is the exercise of His prerogative to use His unlimited power to reflect His divine glory and accomplish His sovereign will. (Matthew 19:26)

K. The Wisdom of God—The wisdom of God refers to His unique ability to so interrelate His attributes that He accomplishes His predetermined purposes by the best means possible. (James 3:13-18)

L. The Veracity of God—The veracity of God means He is always reliable and cannot lie. (Hebrews 6:16-18)

M. The Goodness of God—The goodness of God refers to the collective perfection of His nature and benevolence of His acts. (Psalm 107:1-15)

N. The Wrath of God—The wrath of God is His necessary righteous retribution against sin. (Romans 5:8-9)

O. The Love of God—The love of God is His joyful self-determination to reflect the goodness of His will and glory by meeting the needs of mankind. (1 John 4:7-21)

P. The Grace of God—The grace of God refers to His inexhaustible supply of goodness that does for mankind what they could never do for themselves. (Ephesians 2:1-10)

Q. The Immutability of God—The immutability of God means He never alters His purposes or changes His nature. (Malachi 3:6)

YOUR *Eternity* IS OUR *Priority*

At The Urban Alternative, eternity is our priority—for the individual, the family, the church and the nation. The 45-year teaching ministry of Tony Evans has allowed us to reach a world in need with:

The Alternative – Our flagship radio program brings hope and comfort to an audience of millions on over 1,300 radio outlets across the country.

tonyevans.org – Our library of teaching resources provides solid Bible teaching through the inspirational books and sermons of Tony Evans.

Tony Evans Training Center – Experience the adventure of God's Word with our online classroom, providing at-your-own-pace courses for your PC or mobile device.

Tony Evans app – Packed with audio and video clips, devotionals, Scripture readings and dozens of other tools, the mobile app provides inspiration on-the-go.

Explore God's kingdom today. Live for more than the moment.

Live for *eternity.*

tonyevans.org